rosby, Stills, Nash & Young

BY JOHNNY ROGAN

Copyright © 1998 Johnny Rogan

Edited by Robert Dimery

Cover & Book designed by Hilite Design & Reprographics Limited

Picture research b

ISBN: 0.711

Order No: C

Exclusive Dis

Book Sales Limited, 8/9 Frith St
Music Sales Corporation, 257 Park Avenu
Five Mile Press, 22 Summit Road, No

To the Music

Music Sales Limited, 8/9, Frith Street, London W1V 5TZ, UK.

Photo credits: All pictures supplied by LFI.

Every effort has been made to trace the copyright holders of the photographs in this book but one or two were
unreachable. We would be grateful if the photographers concerned would contact us.

Printed in Great Britain by Printwise (Haverhill) Limited, Suffolk

A catalogue record for this book is available from the British Library.

Visit Omnibus Press at http://www.musicsales.co.uk

OMNIBUS PRESS
LONDON · NEW YORK · SYDNEY

CONTENTS

INTRODUCTION

With such a rich collection of releases to cover in this limited format, there is no time to waste on lengthy introductions. Suffice to say, this is a track by track analysis of every song recorded on officially released albums by Crosby, Stills & Nash, Crosby, Stills, Nash & Young, Stephen Stills, David Crosby, Graham Nash, Crosby & Nash, Manassas and The Stills-Young Band. The releases are logged in chronological order, unfolding the kaleidoscopic interaction of the foursome over nearly 30 years. Compilations are treated separately at the end of the text. Release dates throughout refer to the original US issue; catalogue numbers have been omitted as several of the works cited here have yet to be released in the CD format.

Solo recordings by Neil Young can be found in the 176-page companion volume in this series in which I also detail the complete Buffalo Springfield catalogue. Those seeking more information are advised to consult my other books: *Crosby, Stills, Nash & Young: The Visual Documentary* and, specifically for David Crosby, *The Byrds: Timeless Flight Revisited – The Sequel* (the latter available from PO Box 12728, London SW1P4FB).

JOHNNY ROGAN

CROSBY, STILLS & NASH

CROSBY, STILLS & NASH

CROSBY, STILLS & NASH

ORIGINAL RELEASE DATE: JUNE 1969

Unlike most of the other so-called supergroups of the late Sixties/early Seventies, Crosby, Stills & Nash was a genuine musical union, rather than some inflated jamming session. Their vocal combination was unique, their songwriting articulate, their arrangements inventive and original, and their playing top-notch. The superlative quality of their debut album and alignment with the Woodstock generation captured the imagination of the public at a crucial moment. This album was the definitive example of their vocal and songwriting power and one of the most influential albums of the late Sixties. Despite the supergroup appellation, there was nothing artificial, distant or remote about the music. What they offered was some of the strongest songs of their time, a fascinating combination of political and personal statements that won them a devoted following among critics and public alike. Their music, at once innovative and traditional, forged a link with their antecedents – the Hollies, the Byrds, the Buffalo Springfield – yet ultimately sounded like none of those groups. When CS&N told the world that they were not a group but a union of musical friends who would only get together when they chose and under their own terms, few believed them. Remarkably, every word they said turned out to be true as their kaleidoscopic history so forcibly underlines.

SUITE: JUDY BLUE EYES

Stephen Stills' lengthy, anguished paean to Judy Collins was one of the most dramatic and ambitious opening tracks of any debut album in pop history. The studied, poetic lyrics, striking high harmonies and interweaving acoustic guitars provided a sonic warmth that was simultaneously arresting, soothing and refreshingly new. Although the trio's work as individual composers in their previous groups may have been known to many listeners, no one was prepared for anything this sparkling or innovative. There was a magical blend in the singing and playing that was instantly recognisable yet strikingly original. The ever-ambitious Stills had adapted the song into a suite from a notebook full of extended verses he had composed about his fraught relationship with Collins. "It was the result of a very personal experience that took place over a period of months," he recalled. "It started off as a huge, long narrative poem, which just poured out of me... I happened on a melody and the words that came to mind were from that poem, so I went back to the poem and started picking out pieces. That poem changes in form, so I could only fit part of it to the melody – and I had to write an entirely different melody for other parts where the metre changes." With the song heading for the seven-minute mark, Stills was concerned that the heart-rending mid-section might prove too melodramatic and downcast without an uplifting finale. For this he reverted to his Latin American musical roots to pluck an exuberant ending, which would be indelibly imprinted as CSN's signature melody. As he concluded: "The little kicker at the end about Cuba was just to liven it up because it had gone on forever and I didn't want it to just fall apart. I said: 'Now that we've sung all these lyrics about one thing, let's change the subject entirely.' And we did. Even did it in a different language just to make sure that nobody could understand it."

MARRAKESH EXPRESS

Here was the commercial appeal of the Hollies transposed to CS&N, resulting in the group's first hit single. In different circumstances, the Manchester group might have issued the single themselves, but their resistance to Nash's more ambitious material proved crucial in his decision to leave them. As Nash explained, this evocative composition documented a trip from Casablanca to Marrakesh that he undertook with his wife Rose in 1966. "Every line in that song is true," he noted. "We were sharing a cabin with American ladies five foot tall in blue. We were in the first-class cabin. But I, as always, would go and wander. And I wandered back to the back of the train where there were people in djellebas, lighting fires, and they had pigs and ducks and chickens and goats and straw... I was open enough to react to the circumstances and lucky enough to be in the right place for this melody to come through." When Nash returned to England, he played the songs for the Hollies, who reluctantly attempted it in the studio , before rejecting the track. "After a couple of months of that a man is liable to go insane, especially being the only one who was smoking grass at the time," Nash quipped. Incidentally, the drummer on this track was

not Dallas Taylor, who played on the other songs which required percussion, but session player Jim Gordon.

GUINNEVERE

Crosby's complex composition was one of many highlights on this album. The Arthurian romance elements proved the perfect setting for his romantic tribute to his two great loves of the period, Christine Hinton and Joni Mitchell. Although Crosby has never mentioned her specifically, it is likely that a third girlfriend Nancy Marthai Ross inspired the line about "drawing pentagrams". "They were all archetypes blended into an ethereal one," Crosby remarked of the three women who inspired the composition. Musically, the song was as mysterious and intriguing as its theme, with Crosby switching time signatures to create a jazzy, haunting feel. As he noted: "The thing that surprised me was that I wrote it without having any plan as to how it should happen, and somebody showed me afterwards that it goes 4/4, 6/8, 7/4 each verse. And I went, 'It does?' I didn't know."

YOU DON'T HAVE TO CRY

Another composition born of Stephen Stills' doomed romance with Judy Collins, this was the first song that the trio played together. During an impromptu singing session in Laurel Canyon, Nash witnessed the startling vocal blend and songwriting power of the Crosby/Stills partnership. After listening to this song, he asked them to play the tune once more, then added a high harmony, much to the amazement of everyone present. "Crosby and me just looked at one another," Stills enthused. "It was one of those moments." The song itself was deceptively simple, starting with a traditional folk opening: "In the morning when you rise..." Ostensibly a lyric of fractured romance, there is a surprisingly strong note of petulance and one-upmanship in the lyrics, during which Stills questions female careerism and expresses his own hurt in terms of an emotional powerplay, which is quite intriguing. "It was a letter that never got sent," Stills noted, confirming the strongly autobiographical theme . "I took bits and pieces of it, put them into a song and it got posted through the record business instead of the mail."

PRE-ROAD DOWNS

Swirling organ and reversed-taped guitar, both played by Stills, dominate Nash's sketch of life on the road. An uncredited Cass Elliott makes a surprise appearance on the harmonies, appropriate since she was the person most responsible for bringing the trio together. Nash can probably claim some credit for introducing the word "roaches" to drug innocents the world over.

WOODEN SHIPS

One of the most famous of early CS&N compositions, this apocalyptic tale was written on Crosby's boat, the Mayan. Earlier tapes confirm that he had the melody and basic song written long before 1969, but it was not until Stills came down from New York that they began working on some suitable lyrics, assisted by Paul Kantner, who was uncredited on the original album due to publishing politics. The song begins like a spoken word play with Crosby and Stills playing the part of holocaust survivors. Crosby remembers borrowing the lines "If you smile at me I will understand/Because that is something everybody everywhere does in the same language" from a sign outside a Baptist church in Florida. The scene then moves to an unspecified territory where a new society is evolving in isolation from the "silver people on the shoreline", which was an allusion to the militia in their radiation suits. With Stills adding the expressive lead guitar and dramatic organ breaks, the song had a strong momentum ensuring its place as classic encore material. Before even completing the composition, Stills convinced everybody that it would make a great science fiction movie. "When I first said that it could be a real story, David thought I was crazy," he joked. "It took three days of telling the story for it to sink in. Then we all started making up bits." Crosby loved the anecdotal fashion in which the song developed, explaining: "It's about these guys who survive something – an accidental war – one of our modern wonders... Anyway, they survive and they run into each other in the woods and instead of knocking each other off – which, of course, is what people are supposed to do –

accidentally, one of them smiles at the other. So they decide to be friends and they band together and survive... They work out a language and music and decide that they dig each other and after a while they love each other and start to get it on and they ride off into the sunset." Over the next year there would be much talk of a 'Wooden Ships' movie, with science fiction writer Theodore Sturgeon supposedly providing the script. Unfortunately, the idea remained unrealized.

LADY OF THE ISLAND

This one-take song revealed Nash at his most sparse and intimate, with a tale that mixed romanticism with a strong hint of erotica. He sings alone until the third verse when Crosby and Stills add some quaint harmony. According to Nash the mystery lady of the title was based on two people and there were also two islands: Ibiza and Long Island.

HELPLESSLY HOPING

This was, in many respects, a CS&N primer, complete with scarcely believable three-part harmonies and a subtle acoustic accompaniment. They seldom sounded better than this.

Lyrically, the song was a clever exercise in alliteration. As Stills explained: "I'd started to write a song and after I'd done the first line I remembered an English Language exam in high school. There was a question that went something like, 'Explain and exemplify alliteration'. I got to thinking and I thought I'd write the whole song as a study in alliteration."

LONG TIME GONE

Written on the evening of Bobby Kennedy's assassination, this was one of the great compositions of counter-culture unrest, and a song that was later deemed suitable to open the movie *Woodstock*. The actual recording was a tortuous affair, with Stills and Dallas Taylor working around the clock to complete the bass, organ and guitar parts. The result was nothing less than one of the most powerful songs in the entire CS&N canon. Crosby's bluesy vocal was a revelation, especially considering his previously unsuccessful attempt to sing hard lead on the Byrds' 'Hey Joe'. Here, the passion and feeling spill forth in an intense growl which sounds as though it has drained

Crosby vocally and emotionally. After the recording, he was ecstatic about the results. "I finally found my voice," he exclaimed. "Five years I've been singing and I finally found a voice of my own. Every time I sang a lead in the Byrds I choked up because I was so scared. But these two cats loved me enough to let me find my own voice." An amusing footnote to the 'Long Time Gone' story was the enduring memory of Crosby and company singing along with Tom Jones on the song on his television show in October 1969. Crosby was later mortified by the memory, but Stills quipped: "I really dig Tom Jones... he's got incredible chops".

49 BYE-BYES

The album closes with two Stills songs, '49 Reasons' and 'Bye Bye Baby', combined into one. There is almost a nursery rhyme element to the opening, "49 reasons all in a line", before the song moves into a rugged tale of romance on the plains. Stills employs Western imagery with the references to a drifter who seduces a capricious woman whose role in the story is occasionally reduced to the level of a prize in a card game ("I let that man play his hand"). As we move into the 'Bye Bye Baby' section, the pace and tempo quicken along with Stills' shifting sentiments, which swiftly alter from hurt pride to renewed arrogance as he taunts the feckless woman before concluding with a final flourish of defiant optimism ("Time will tell us, who is trying to sell us"), punctuated by a reverberating instrumental coda. A fascinating end to a remarkable album.

Crosby, Stills, Nash & Young
Dallas Taylor & Greg Reeves

Déjà vu

CROSBY STILLS, NASH & YOUNG

DÉJÀ VU

ORIGINAL RELEASE DATE: MARCH 1970

Neil Young's modest recording career took a decisive turn in 1969 when he was invited to join Crosby, Stills & Nash. They were already receiving premature plaudits as the most promising and accomplished ensemble of their era, a view reinforced by the quality of their debut album. If ever the word "supergroup" meant anything, then CSN&Y were worthy recipients. Young brought a keener edge to their music and his electric interchanges with Stills were spectacular to behold. Although CS&N could have recruited a sideman of quality who was not a songwriter they unselfishly allowed Young the chance to present his material to an audience that he might never have reached playing with Crazy Horse or singing solo.

This album looked like the start of a long and rewarding partnership but, frustratingly, it was to prove only one of two CSN&Y studio albums and its follow-up would not appear until as late as 1988. Much has been made of the fact that the foursome didn't appear together on every track but there was nothing unusual about that in rock music at the time. What is important is that the album had an aural unity, sounding like nothing else that had preceded it both in terms of production and performance. It was widely and wildly celebrated in the UK and established the foursome as kings of rock in the USA where it topped the charts. Young's influence on the album was strong, which is one of the reasons why you miss him so much on later CS&N releases. Nevertheless, he was never in a position to dominate the quartet, whose songwriting efforts were generally equal and occasionally superior to his own. At this point, the foursome seemed to have everything but that superiority merely encouraged them to pursue related projects, ultimately to the detriment of the dream team, whose impermanence was part of their mystical appeal.

CARRY ON

Stephen Stills' 'Carry On' opened the album on a note of technical mastery. The spine-tingling harmonies still impress, even after years of listening to paltry imitations by scores of other artistes. Considerable time went into the acoustic and electric segments of the song until Stills the perfectionist was satisfied. At this point in his career, Stills was a great technician who loved to synthesize different ideas. 'Carry On' was actually three tracks combined to make a single song. Part of the backing track was an instrumental jam that Stills and Dallas Taylor had been working on; the 'Questions' segment was borrowed from the Buffalo Springfield song of the same title, and the remainder was written during a break between sessions. Recalling its completion, Stills explained: "We needed an opener for the album so I went back to the motel and wrote a song about how the group was then... our session scene at 7 pm

to 7 am. We stuck the song on the front of a little jam which our drummer Dallas Taylor and I had worked out three nights before."

TEACH YOUR CHILDREN

Nash's injunction to parents was originally conceived as a folk tune until Stills elected to "make it swing" by providing a more upbeat arrangement. The track was given added sparkle by the inclusion of The Grateful Dead's Jerry Garcia on steel guitar. At the time, the song was regarded by many, including the other members of CSN&Y, as Nash's best post-Hollies' composition. An effusive Stephen Stills even went as far as calling it, "the best track on the album, head and shoulders above the rest." When asked to name his best ever song, Nash concurred, adding with true Sixties' idealism: " 'Teach Your Children' because it's the only answer. Children are the only answer in this world because we have all been children and why we're all screwed up is that we've been conditioned. If we can condition children differently and give them different values and make them more real, then that eventually will save everything."

ALMOST CUT MY HAIR

In common with 'Long Time Gone', this song was written by Crosby on the night that Robert Kennedy was assassinated. At the time of its release, the song divided the critics; some felt that it was excessive in its ranting, while others recognized that it was one of Crosby's most passionate and heart-felt performances. Even the playing and singing on the track were subjects of heated debate, with Stills arguing that they could have achieved a better take than the one that appears on the record. As Crosby explained: "I kept 'Almost Cut My Hair' in there over the protestations of Stephen, who didn't want me to leave it in because he thought that it was a bad vocal. And it was a bad vocal in the sense that it slid around and it wasn't polished, but I felt like what I meant when I sang it, and so it always put me on that trip. Now, I don't know whether that communicated to the people out there or not... I don't know whether it communicated anything but just a bunch of raucous guitar and me yelling. If it did communicate, then it was right." Over the years, Crosby's instinctive feelings were vindicated and later critics, backed by no less a personage than Neil Young, pointed out that the one-take method adopted by Crosby here gave the song a force and spontaneity refreshing amid their other elaborately produced compositions. "It was all of us playing and singing at the same time," Crosby revealed. "It was a very tough time for me. It was right after Christine got killed and I was not my best as a functioning person. I would sometimes come into the studio and end up crying being unable to deal with it."

He would cut the tracks by himself. Then he would arrange them vocally and sing them." Young recalled having to cajole CS&N into playing the way he liked. " 'Helpless' was a slow song," he remembered. "I had to play it with them until four o'clock in the morning, doing it over and over and over again to get everybody too tired enough so that they would stop doing this extra stuff where everyone was playing too much. We kept on going for a long time. Finally, we got one where they were half-asleep and they didn't know they were doing it."

HELPLESS

Young's nostalgic vision of Omenee, Ontario betrayed an unusually stoical tone as though it was written as a pastoral panacea to the problems of his present day life as an emerging rock star. CS&N provided a memorably strong harmonic blend with Crosby, as ever, adding depth to the melody. " 'Helpless' is real emotional," Crosby told me. "I liked the harmonies and the overall power of the thing. However, I thought it was unfortunate that he did his songs so much by himself. He wouldn't let us have much to do with them.

WOODSTOCK

Stephen Stills had originally planned to write a tribute to the Woodstock Festival, but ended up arranging an electric version composed by Joni Mitchell. "We played at Woodstock and it really blew our minds," he recalled. "On the plane back, I was trying hard to think of something to write about the festival. We told Joni of our plans and I kept working out some ideas. Just as I was on the verge of getting it together, Joni came over and played us her song. She got there first. I said I couldn't top it." The distinctive CSN&Y

electric guitar work gave the song a strong separate identity from the more reflective chart-topping cover by Matthews' Southern Comfort. However, Neil Young later suggested that an even better version was passed over because they felt it was too raw and spontaneous. An alternate version of the song was played over the closing credits of the film *Woodstock*.

DÉJÀ VU

Crosby's love of unusual time signatures was clearly evident on the title track, which proved the most difficult song to complete, logging close to a hundred hours in studio time. "To me, 'Déjà Vu' was the whole second album," Stills concluded. "It's kind of the summation of what 'Carry On' said and what 'Teach Your Children' said and all of those songs. 'Déjà Vu' said it all." The song also inspired the evocative album sleeve with CSN&Y and sidemen Greg Reeves and Dallas Taylor dressed in American Civil War period costume. The sensation of "Déjà Vu" was felt very strongly by Crosby during the period of writing the work. "It came out of a very distinct feeling

that the reincarnation thing had felt like it was real," he told Paul Zollo of *Song Talk*. "There's things in my life that I can't explain any other way. I knew how to sail a boat the first time I saw one. I was 11 and I got into a sailboat and I knew how to do it... same thing as singing. I started singing harmony when I was six. You're not supposed to know how to do that. And I've always instinctively known where to go with music and songs."

OUR HOUSE

Nash's sentimental, idyllic portrayal of living with Joni Mitchell in Laurel Canyon sounded like a hippie version of Coventry Patmore's *The Angel In The House*. "It was written on her piano," Nash recalled. "Such a charming house. She had a collection of multi-coloured glass in a window that would catch the light – the 'fiery gems'. There was a fireplace and two cats in the yard. It was like a family snapshot, a portrait of our life together." Ironically, the song would be later be employed as a television advertisement by the Halifax Building Society.

4+20

This was originally intended for inclusion on Stills' first solo album but once his fellow members heard the song they insisted it be added to *Déjà Vu*. Sparse, dramatically concise and extraordinarily moving in its stark admission of desolation, the song remains one of Stills' most expressive and unheralded compositions. The intimacy of the performance suggests that the sentiments were autobiographical, a view reinforced by the title and the date of composition, which was just after Stills' 24th birthday. However, according to the composer the song was "about an 84-year-old poverty stricken man who started and finished with nothing." How Stills manages to make 4 plus 20 equal 84, however, remains a mathematical mystery.

COUNTRY GIRL

The power of Young's work with CS&N was seldom bettered than in this remarkable composition which was actually an amalgam of three song segments. Strongly influenced by Jack Nitzsche, it demonstrated Young's determination to emulate Phil Spector with a grandiose production. The results are magnificent with CS&N excelling themselves as the perfect back-up group. Regrettably, this represented the scale of Young's artistic ambition as a member of CSN&Y and he never again attempted an epic to match this singular achievement.

EVERYBODY I LOVE YOU

Two separate songs were fused together for this composition: Stills' 'Know You Got To Run' and Young's 'Everybody I Love You'. What emerged was a fast-paced, vibrant finale for this much loved album. In the final 30 seconds or so, Young receives a salutary lesson from CS&N and is buried beneath their vocal power. Stills' blues phrasing and Crosby/Nash's skyward harmonies interfuse in what can only be described as an almost too perfect studio creation, culminating in what sounds like a full blown church organ. As a wilful practitioner of the imperfect, Young failed to appreciate the technical and emotional strengths that the superstar trio brought to his songs. Despite all his later genre experiments, he never returned to the full scale Spectoresque productions that characterized his now severely and unfairly underrated work with CS&N.

STEPHEN STILLS

STEPHEN STILLS

STEPHEN STILLS

ORIGINAL RELEASE DATE: NOVEMBER 1970

One of the greatest of albums in the entire CSN&Y canon, this was the work that established Stephen Stills' reputation as one of the most inventive and multi-talented musicians of his era. Always competitive, he seemed determined to transcend the achievements of the CSN&Y collective by unveiling a work that fully demonstrated his reputation as rock's most celebrated Renaissance man. At the time of the record's release, he had already been hailed by San Francisco's premier music critic Ralph Gleason as "one of the best lyric songwriters in all of contemporary music". This album vindicated that statement with a series of songs whose eclecticism was quite astonishing. While the work featured a number of heavyweight helpers, including Jimi Hendrix, Eric Clapton and Ringo Starr, their presence was always subservient to the power of Stills' songwriting. At this point, Stills was regarded as one of the leading figures in rock, and an even greater force than his former colleague Neil Young. This album was arguably a career best, a triumph of imagination and ambition whose distinctive and original sound still resonates over two-and-a-half decades on.

LOVE THE ONE YOU'RE WITH

The nickname Captain Manyhands was well-earned by Stills as this opening track indicates. He plays organ, guitar, percussion, and even steel drums, requiring only some additional congas from Jeff Whittaker and the sumptuous bass of Fuzzy Samuels to fill out the track. Probably the most famous of Stills' solo songs, this provided him with his only UK Top 40 hit and reached number 14 in the US. Crosby & Nash provided the catchy harmonies, the effect brilliantly reinforced by the presence of John Sebastian, Rita Coolidge and her sister Priscilla Jones. Given CSN&Y's penchant for songs of doomed romanticism, it's interesting to witness Stills taking a more practical, if not expedient, view of relationships. The song's title was borrowed from Billy Preston. As Stills remembers: "I asked him if I could pinch this line he had written for a song, and he said, 'Sure'. So I pinched it and wrote the song. My favourite part is the steel drums. I'd played them before a little but I just kept diddling around till I found the right notes."

DO FOR THE OTHERS

By contrast, this was Stills the acoustic troubadour. "I wanted a folk song for the album, just a very simple song," he explained. Although he had a version of the song complete with overdubbed autoharps and additional instrumentation, he chose to use the original mix recorded during his period living in England. Another impressive composition in the Stills' canon, the song expressed a nobility in the face of emotional turmoil, with the singer suggesting charity as a response to rejection.

CHURCH

Co-arranged with Arif Mardin, this revealed Stills' gospel roots, complete with a church organ and a "bring the house down" chorus. "There's five voices, including mine," Stills explained. "As it originally came out, it was something I really believed in. That's what you sing about in church. I've certainly spent my time in church but I'm not particularly religious. I believe in religion as an ordered form, but I don't think you could quite call me an agnostic. Mother Nature plays the best music and makes the best paintings, it's certainly more powerful than anything we got yet. Could just be that the body is the temple of the Lord." Overall, the song was a testament to Stills' eclecticism, taking the album from pop to folk and gospel over successive tracks.

OLD TIMES, GOOD TIMES

Stills idolized Jimi Hendrix and during this period intended to record a joint album with the guitarist. That dream ended when Hendrix was found dead. Stills was so shaken by the news that he climbed a mountain

and wept for two hours. He subsequently instructed Atlantic Records to add the words "Dedicated to James Marshall Hendrix" to the sleeve of this album, just weeks before its release. This track is a lasting testament to a superb collaboration with Stills singing and playing organ, while Hendrix offers a startling guitar flurry. The familiar choppy bass playing of Fuzzy Samuels interspersed with Jeff Whittaker's congas sets off the track neatly for Hendrix's final break. Recalling the session, Stills revealed: "Hendrix and I cut a bunch of stuff together. This is one of the few things that surfaced. He was a very dear friend of mine. We were lonely in London together and hung out a lot. I left England suddenly, and years later I learned from Mitch Mitchell that Jimi had been looking for me everywhere – wanted me to join the Experience as the bass player, which would have been my greatest dream in life."

GO BACK HOME

Not content with commandeering the talents of Jimi Hendrix, Stills also employed Eric Clapton for this blues/rock workout. The song began slowly as a studied blues with Stills playing basic guitar, keyboards and singing in that familiar gruff voice, while Fuzzy Samuels and drummers Johnny Barbata and Dallas Taylor provided a solid groove. The track culminated in a breathtaking guitar duel between Stills and Clapton, which was even more memorable than those played out with Neil Young in the Buffalo Springfield. While working at Island Studios, Stills reciprocated by playing bass and supplying backing vocals to Clapton's 'Let It Rain'.

SIT YOURSELF DOWN

This was the last song written for the album and another highlight. The track was later issued as a follow-up single to 'Love The One You're With' and provided Stills with his second US Top 40 hit as a soloist. Lyrically, the song talks of the need to settle down, with oblique references to "the Raven", a favourite symbol that Stills occasionally used for Rita Coolidge. There is a sense of manic frustration at the heart of the song as Stills grapples with the frustration of achieving the easy life and pours forth one of his most intense and impassioned vocals. The excitement level is raised tenfold by the remarkable, almost overwhelming chorus provided by the massed ranks of David Crosby, Graham Nash, John Sebastian, Rita Coolidge, Priscilla Jones, Cass Elliott and Claudia Lanier.

TO A FLAME

Recorded in England, with Arif Mardin conducting the orchestra, this was one of Stills' great torch songs. The familiar bird imagery, already employed on songs like 'Bluebird' and 'Suite: Judy Blue Eyes', returns with the references to burned wings following another broken relationship. There's a moment of unintended wry humour when Stills sings, "Lucky for me I'm not a jealous man", a claim hardly vindicated considering the smouldering passion of which he is capable in most of his love songs, this one included. The mid-section, a beautiful orchestral lilt, was neatly complemented by Stills' fluid playing and Ringo Starr's easy-going drumming style. At the end of the song, Stills was stumped for a line to follow the admonition: "Go ahead break your heart but don't fall apart," but eventually came up with the engaging simile: "It's like saying goodbye to Paris for the first time."

BLACK QUEEN

Stills' convincing attempt to transform himself into a Mississippi Delta bluesman was achieved with the aid of copious amounts of Jose Cuervo Gold Label tequila. "I just walked in the studio and did it," Stills remarked of this unique performance. "Before that, Eric Clapton and I had played 'Tequila' for about an hour and a half, and then, all of a sudden, he was gone. He disappeared... He realized that if he didn't go he was going to pass out in the studio, so he got someone to drive him home while he was still able to reach the car." At that point, the inebriated Stills convinced himself that he was a blues singer, ready to record a song about a card game. "I stumbled right into the studio and that's what came out. I had been out to Eric's house the night before listening to Blind Willie Johnson records, and so the vocal quality is 'arrrgh'. You know, it sounds like a saw. It hurts physically. It hurts my throat to sing like that, but it sure does sound neat." The song leaves enduring

images of bleeding fingers and burned larynx, while adding another dimension to Stills' repertoire.

CHEROKEE

Sidney George's flute and exuberant alto saxophone accompaniment transforms this track, which is one of the most exciting on the album. The time shift from 7/4 to 4/4 adds drama to the piece, as Stills relates what is surely a thinly disguised tribute to Rita Coolidge. Booker T. Jones provides the organ, while the ever busy Stills plays lead guitar, bass and vocals, and both writes and arranges the song. The Stax sound experiments with Sidney George would continue in more bombastic fashion on Stills' second solo album.

WE ARE NOT HELPLESS

The title and emphatic opening line, "We are not helpless we are men" suggested to many that this was Stills' answer to Neil Young's fatalistic 'Helpless'. However, this was not the case according to Stephen who claims to have borrowed the line from the novel *Failsafe*. The song itself provided a breathtaking and audacious conclusion to the album, building slowly from an austere acoustic opening to the gradual introduction of organ and some solid drumming, courtesy of Ringo Starr. Stills felt he needed a grand finale and this provided all the answers. The lyrics were valiant and positive, while the deceptively quiet ballad opening transmuted into an extraordinary tour de force, highlighted by a speaker-splitting organ that threatened to swamp the vocal. With Ringo keeping pace, the song moved into a new rhythm as Stills sang his poem 'America's Children', set against a gospel backing. The remarkable choral ending featured the combined voices of Stills, Rita Coolidge, David Crosby, Graham Nash, John Sebastian, Cass Elliott, Priscilla Jones, Claudia Lanier, Booker T. Jones and Shirlie Matthews soaring to the heavens as the organ resonated into infinity. A breathtaking conclusion to an exemplary album.

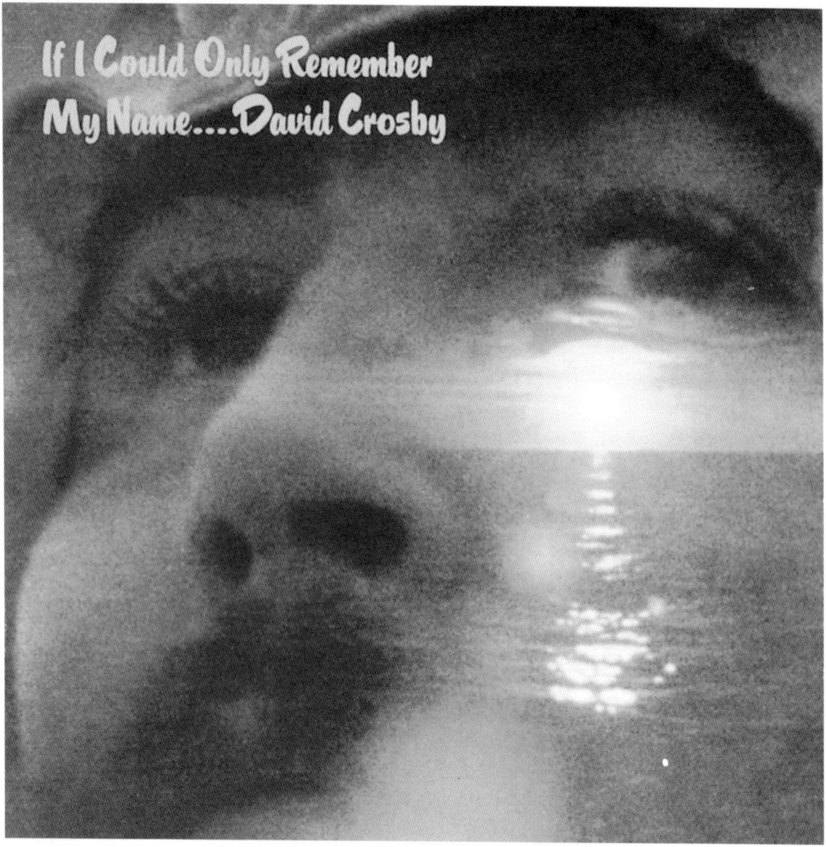
If I Could Only Remember
My Name....David Crosby

DAVID CROSBY

IF I COULD ONLY REMEMBER MY NAME

ORIGINAL RELEASE DATE: MARCH 1971

Crosby's first solo album was released during the golden age of CSN&Y when, for the best part of three years, everything that they released was of exceptional, world-beating quality. Even by their highest standards, this work was exceptional. Here was an album that transcended its time like no other from the period. Rather than composing the expected singer-songwriter album of love-lorn ballads, Crosby daringly produced a striking and experimental mood piece, laced with exquisite harmonies, unusual time signatures and dazzling choral arrangements. More than a solo album with studio guest stars, this was akin to a musical love-in, featuring the cream of the West Coast aristocracy and San Franciscan outlaws. Members of the Grateful Dead, Jefferson Airplane, plus Graham Nash, Neil Young and Joni Mitchell, all became part of the creative process. Much of the record's enduring power came from Crosby's emotional state during the period. Still reeling from the death of his lover Christine Hinton, he set about composing reflective pieces, culminating in a remarkable requiem in which her spirit seemed to enter the studio portals. Throughout the sessions, the accompanying players fed off his emotion and commitment, reaching heights that equalled their best work. Although the album went gold and reached the Top 20 on both sides of the Atlantic, its importance over the years has not always been stated. Yet, this was an album that could not be locked in a time capsule labelled "early Seventies singer-songwriter". Whatever the changing reputation of CSN&Y, this was one work that transcended fashions and prejudices. Today, it sounds as, if not more, extraordinary than it did back in 1971. Its continued high placing in books like *The All-Time Top 1,000 Albums* is a testament to a work which still inclines critics towards reverential and effusive exclamation.

MUSIC IS LOVE

Acoustic guitars meld from each speaker as this understated opening track brilliantly sets the mood for the album. Neil Young's backing vocal combines surprisingly well with Crosby's lead, as the song develops into an irresistible, hypnotic chant. "That was an improvisation," Crosby remembers. "That was a couple of bits I had fooled around with, once or twice, and I was sitting there with Neil and Graham. At that point, we were very experimental. We would go in with no pre-plan and just record stuff... That's a one take improvisational thing that just came out. I said, 'Well, that's fun, now let's get on and do some serious stuff'. And Neil looked at Graham and Graham looked at Neil and they said, 'Sure'. And they took the tape. They stole the tape and added Neil on bass and Graham on conga drums and gave it back to me and said, 'It's going on your record, man. It's really cool. You ought to start with this."

COWBOY MOVIE

This eight-minute track was the longest and most electric cut on the album. Like several of the other songs herein, it builds in intensity and features some staggering playing. An alternate take features Neil Young, but here it is Jerry Garcia providing the blistering guitar work, which reaches new heights at the precise point at which Crosby sings of his character's confrontation with Rita Coolidge in her alias as Raven, the Indian Girl. Coolidge served as something of a catalyst in the CSN&Y story, inspiring songs from Stills, Nash and Crosby. Although this song was generally perceived as a musical western, it was actually an allegory of the quartet's break-up. Stills had been enamoured of Coolidge and written songs about her only to see her romanced away by Nash, a situation that resulted in a serious fall-out, which blighted collaborations for some time thereafter. Interpreted from this angle, the song was more than intriguing. As Crosby explained to me: "That was the story of CSN&Y. You have to know who's who. The Indian Girl? That's Rita Coolidge. Stephen is Eli, our fastest gunner, kind of mean and young from the South. The Duke, the dynamiter, that's Nash. Young Billy, that's Neil. And old, weird Albert with the 12-gauge

– that's me. I smeared my face up with blood from my thumb, lay down on the floor and played real good possum – I'm crazy, but I ain't real dumb. That Indian, she wasn't an Indian, she was the law – the law of how things naturally happen, the law of human nature, the law of averages. At the time that was a factor. It wasn't the only one, but it was a factor. Listen to it now that you know the story."

TAMALPAIS HIGH (AT ABOUT 3)

Mt Tamalpais was one of Crosby's favourite spots for meditation and this choral piece is a superb mood accompaniment, particularly following the drama of the preceding track. Backed by various members of The Grateful Dead, Crosby creates a trippy ambience, set against some exceptional playing. "David's a very giving musician," Jerry Garcia observed. "His songs are special and they're very different, so it's always a challenge to work with him. He's into that loose 'anything goes' creative space, which is especially fun when you're a supporting musician... And the pay-off is when you hear

it back. It sounds beautiful... I think some of the finest playing I've done on record is on his solo album. As far as being personally satisfied with my own performances, which I rarely am, he's gotten better out of me than I get out of myself."

LAUGHING

Originally written with the Byrds in mind, Crosby was fired from the group shortly before completing the work, although he did later manage to include the track on their 1973 reunion album. This earlier version is superior and stands among his best compositions of the period, with exemplary playing and exotic harmonies. Lyrically, this was another of what Crosby called his "Well, gee, who am I? What's going on here? Where's the instruction booklet? How come nobody knows what's going on? songs". The final verse in which he momentarily discovers a guru who is exposed as a child laughing in the sun was a line inspired by George Harrison's devotion to the Maharishi Mahesh Yogi. For engineer Stephen Barncard, "This was the most magical track of all; it happened so fast. Joni Mitchell made her guest appearance here on backing vocals ("In the sun"), while the other musicians featured were Jerry Garcia (pedal steel), Phil Lesh (bass) and Bill Kreutzmann (tambourine and drums)."

WHAT ARE THEIR NAMES

Despite the relative brevity of this song it boasted a five-way writing credit: Crosby, Neil Young, Jerry Garcia, Phil Lesh and Michael Shrieve. Commencing with some delicate picking the song builds slowly but dramatically as more instruments intrude, culminating in an unforgettable vocal climax, with Grace Slick soaring in the background. The sudden recruitment of a full-scale chorus almost wrong-footed engineer Stephen Barncard, who had to act quickly to capture the big moment. "I didn't have much time to do it," he remembered. "Maybe a 10-minute window to record all these people: Joni Mitchell, Grace Slick, Paul Kantner, David, Graham, David Freiberg, Jerry Garcia, Phil Lesh, Bob Weir, maybe Mickey Hart and Spencer Dryden too. Immediately, I have to figure out how do I get enough headphones to get all of these people covered? In 10 minutes? No way. So, I put a bunch of mikes out there and bussed them together and then put the track out in the speakers. That gave it a sort of washed-out effect, but I brought up all the faders on the board and made one or two runs; out of an impossible situation we got a spontaneous, timeless track. Once I burned through my frustration at the technical level, what I found was that if you let the music do the magic work, amazing things can happen."

TRACTION IN THE RAIN

This was one of Crosby's most enchanting compositions of the period, enhanced wonderfully by Laura Allen on zither. The evocative lyrics were inspired by a near altercation that occurred when Crosby was in the company of Joan Baez and her sister Mimi Farina. "There were some anti-protester protesters," he recalled, "young guys who were ticked off because we were hippie scum and we were walking with beautiful girls and they weren't. The T-shirt in the song was turning green with envy and the olive branch was there because we were peaceniks." Complementing the expressive lyrics was some precise acoustic playing and a stylish Crosby vocal that added to the ethereal feel. As Jerry Garcia perceptively noted: "Crosby has never gotten the credit he deserves. He's an uncanny singer. He has as much control as anybody I've seen or worked with. He can do things that are truly astonishing if you give him half a chance and when he has his own head and he's in good shape, boy, he's fun to work with. He's an inspiration."

SONG WITH NO WORDS (TREE WITH NO LEAVES)

This was one of Crosby's most melancholic or uplifting reflections, depending upon the mood of the listener. The harmonic blend with Nash was spinechilling, while the subtle use of instrumentation, including electric/acoustic guitars (Crosby, Garcia and Kaukonen) and piano (Greg Rolie), was mixed deep in order to complement the transcendent mood. The composition was a major achievement and a rare but salutary example of how a work can sometimes benefit by the exclusion of lyrics. "When I wrote this song, it seemed complete," Crosby

noted. "It never asked me for words. It felt good, so I left it that way... Nash dubbed it 'Tree With No Leaves'. Early on a lot of people made much of my music being strange because I used a lot of odd tunings, and the fact that my songs often didn't follow the usual cyclical, short and easy repeat patterns – which is one reason I was thrilled when I met Nash. He understood my stuff the first minute he heard it. Nash has never been puzzled by my music, ever. The farthest out thing I ever tried to do, Nash just went, 'Yeah, sure'. The tunings I use I hit on by fooling around with other guitar players, and experimenting. The way we all got into it was tuning the bottom E string down to D. That was the first one everybody did. The next thing you tried was tuning the top E string down to D also, which Stephen loves, a modal tuning. In 'Song With No Words'... the A is up a whole tone to B, B is down a whole tone to A, and the high E is down a whole tone to D."

ORLEANS

Crosby's multi-vocal hymnal version of this traditional number was as haunting as the rest of the album with some excellently played acoustic guitars augmenting the track. David was introduced to the song by Paul Kantner and the lyrics refer to the names of cathedrals in France. Perfectly placed on the album, it sets the mood for the climactic requiem that follows.

I'D SWEAR THERE WAS SOMEBODY HERE

This eerie finale, akin to a Gregorian chant, was conceived and created in the studio during a moment of transcendence. "It was like a bolt of lightning," engineer Stephen Barncard remembered. "I've rarely seen anything that intense... It just happened. I witnessed the creation of the song in real time and recorded it as we went along. It was probably the most remarkable event in my entire life." Barncard's hyperbole was justified as there has seldom, if ever, been a more chilling and unforgettable climax to an album in the genre.

CROSBY, STILLS, NASH & YOUNG

4 WAY STREET

ORIGINAL RELEASE DATE: APRIL 1971

This live double album soon emulated the chart achievements of *Déjà Vu* by climbing to number 1 in the US charts. Surprisingly, *Rolling Stone* nominated the work as CS&N/CSN&Y's best yet, marvelling with pained condescension that they "all sing and play in the same key on almost every cut". With Neil Young having just hit big with *After The Goldrush*, he gained most of the critical plaudits that were handed out. The evident bias was not matched by the material which clearly showed that the other three were more than a match for him at this point. Against all odds, it was Crosby & Nash who rose to the occasion by performing the only previously unissued songs in the set. David's 'The Lee Shore' was one of his most beautiful sea songs, with evocative imagery and a sumptuous arrangement. There was also a surprise new reading of 'Triad', his *menage à trois* composition that the Jefferson Airplane had recorded after the Byrds coolly rejected the song. Crosby prefaced the performance with an intimate explanation of the writing process. Nash also showed taste with his new offering 'Right Between The Eyes'. The exuberant Stills was on equally good form throughout and provided the set with its most arresting and humorous excursion in the medley of '49 Bye Byes/For What It's Worth', which culminated in a thumping tirade in which he denounced Spiro Agnew and Richard Daley and even equated pacifism with political revolution by informing us that "Jesus Christ was the first non-violent revolutionary – dig it". Young was well represented but more restrained throughout and there were no new compositions from him for fans to savour. Instead, we were treated to some intriguing rearrangements of older material as Young adapted to his new role as a purveyor of CS&N-style "wooden music". Buffalo Springfield's now dated pop version of 'On The Way Home' became a favourite opening number, fitting unobtrusively into his acoustic repertoire. Even more surprising was 'Cowgirl In The Sand' now translated from electric epic glory into a compact ballad. By contrast, the recent 'Don't Let It Bring You Down' replicated the mood of the studio version.

The electric side was staunch, following the trends of the period by featuring elongated workouts of familiar songs. Young contributed a far longer version of 'Southern Man' than the one on *After The Goldrush* and Stills followed suit with 'Carry On'. The Stills/Young jams seemed a tad over indulgent, though it should be remembered that such extended workouts were then all the rage. Completing the Young contributions on the original disc was 'Ohio', already issued as a single and rightly acclaimed as the peak of CSN&Y's achievement. The live version could not hope to match the economy and emotional intensity of the original but nevertheless provided some indication of the power of the composition when played live. Crosby's 'Long Time Gone' was more restrained than the work of his fellow guitarists and was complimented by several critics for its power and intensity.

When *4 Way Street* was finally issued on compact disc, several new acoustic tracks were added, including Crosby's 'Laughing', Nash's reinterpretation of the Hollies' classic 'King Midas In Reverse', an intense 'Black Queen' and Young's engaging medley of 'The Loner/Cinnamon Girl/Down By The River'. As a memento of the quartet's illustrious indoor concerts of 1970, this package retains an enduring charm.

Full track listing: Suite: Judy Blue Eyes; On The Way Home; Teach Your Children; Triad; The Lee Shore; Chicago; Right Between The Eyes; Cowgirl In The Sand; Don't Let It Bring You Down; 49 Bye-Byes/America's Children; Love The One You're With; Pre-Road Downs; Long Time Gone; Southern Man; Ohio; Carry On; Find The Cost Of Freedom. The CD version features the following additional tracks: King Midas In Reverse; Laughing; Black Queen and Medley: The Loner/Cinnamon Girl/Down By The River.

SONGS FOR BEGINNERS
GRAHAM NASH

GRAHAM NASH

SONGS FOR BEGINNERS

ORIGINAL RELEASE DATE: MAY 1971

Graham Nash's debut solo album may have lacked the depth of Crosby and Stills' first solo efforts, but unquestionably established his claim to be a serious singer songwriter. At times, he appeared to be trying almost too hard, with over-earnest lyrics and lines that occasionally stumbled into self-absorption. The wide-eyed utopianism, simple didacticism and overt sentimentality of Nash's observations were very much of their time, as was that peculiar mixture of ego and vulnerability at the heart of his lyrics. As a grouping of Nash songs, however, this was pretty strong and included several of his best compositions. Interestingly, no less a personage than Neil Young's manager Elliot Roberts maintained that this was the best of the immediate post *Déjà Vu* solo albums by CSN&Y, which was no small compliment considering the brilliance of the competition.

MILITARY MADNESS

Nash's autobiographical account of his birth and subsequent emigration to America is paralleled by the omnipresence of war. Dave Mason's wah-wah guitar enlivens the track, while Rita Coolidge and P. P. Arnold provide the soulful backing vocals. Crosby & Nash usually ended their acoustic concerts with this singalong during the early Seventies and 20 years later CS&N opened theirs with the same song.

BETTER DAYS

With Nash on piano, augmented by Joe Yankee (an alias for Neil Young), this stoical acoustic ballad was one of Graham's more soul-searching reflections. The track was given even greater momentum by an impressive bass clarinet solo by Seemon

Posthuma. Nash had recently co-produced Seemon and Marijke's *Son Of America*, which was released during this same period.

WOUNDED BIRD

This stark ballad was an uneasy attempt at reconciling pride and humility, with Nash singing alone, although his voice is double-tracked in places. There is a didactic tone to Nash's sentiments which detracts somewhat from his protestations of vulnerability.

I USED TO BE A KING

With The Grateful Dead's Phil Lesh on bass and Jerry Garcia on piano and steel guitar, this proved one of the most powerful tracks on the album. The title neatly echoed The Hollies' 'King Midas In Reverse', while Nash also namechecked Buffalo Springfield's 'For What It's Worth'. His steely abnegation of romance was sung with considerable passion.

BE YOURSELF

With lover Rita Coolidge on electric and acoustic piano, Nash offered another song of self-realization, this time translated into a rallying call, complete with an unnamed chorus.

SIMPLE MAN

Nash's bemused response to the loss of Joni Mitchell was captured in this self-effacing song written during the afternoon of 4 July 1970, prior to CSN&Y's opening performance at the Fillmore. Dorian Rudaytsky plays the haunting cello, while Nash disguises a strong ego with a disingenuous humility.

MAN IN THE MIRROR

Like many of the other songs on the album, this was written during a period of self-imposed isolation at the Chateau Marmont in which Nash meditated on the darker aspects of superstar life. Neil Young, in his Joe Yankee persona, again appeared on piano, with Jerry Garcia providing the striking steel guitar.

THERE'S ONLY ONE

An interesting arrangement, including a great sax solo by Bobby Keys. Nash's lyrics betrayed an almost adolescent portentousness here, switching uneasily to the plural as he attempted to universalize his own experiences. The simple rhyme scheme (a-a-b-b) was no doubt intended to cut through political and economic complexities and allow the earnest Nash to set out an easily understood agenda calling for social equality.

SLEEP SONG

Nash adds a paper and comb accompaniment to his repertoire on this simple and overly personal glimpse into his bedroom. The lyrics had a nursery rhyme quality with a hint of eroticism, but there was also a mawkishness to the sentiments in some of the lines.

CHICAGO/WE CAN CHANGE THE WORLD

This was partly written as a plea to Stills and Young to play a benefit gig for the Chicago Seven. They declined. The song originally featured in several CSN&Y concerts as a stark but powerful acoustic number and was captured as such on the live album, *4 Way Street*. This electric version provided a suitable climax to the album, with a battalion of backing singers, including Rita Coolidge, Vanetta Fields, Shirley Matthews, Clydie King and Dorothy Morrison.

STEPHEN STILLS 2

STEPHEN STILLS

STEPHEN STILLS 2

ORIGINAL RELEASE DATE: JUNE 1971

Although strong, Stills' second album lacked the consistent excellence of its predecessor. There were occasional lapses into maudlin self-indulgence as Stills threatened to topple his fragile songs into bathos with epical arrangements and big brass workouts. Fortunately, the general standard of the songs was excellent and Stills was happy to try something new. "I was really trying to come to grips with becoming an arranger – a real one," he told reporter Penny Valentine at the time. "I was writing charts for strings and horns and that really is the whole trip with the big band... I dig it and it's groovy and there's some of this that's overdone a bit too. It doesn't really matter, I'm happy." Any chance of Stills continuing the big brass arrangements ended when he took the Memphis Horns on a US tour most notable for his tortured, drunken performances at several dates. Still recovering from an ill-fated relationship, he turned to the bottle and by the end of the tour was ready for something new.

CHANGE PARTNERS

Chiming guitars introduce Stills' charming song of Southern gentility, with Crosby & Nash adding some strong harmonies. The dance motif also served as a subtext for the various shifts in personnel in the CSN&Y story. Although Stills was inspired by attending debutante balls in his younger days, he too came to see the song's wider significance in later years.

NOTHIN' TO DO BUT TODAY

Fiery blues and well-executed harmonies characterized this song, but its real power emanated from the fluid guitar work of Eric Clapton which gave the track an extra edge.

FISHES AND SCORPIONS

Switching from acoustic to electric guitar in successive verses, Stills offered some astrological fun, no doubt with Rita Coolidge's star sign in there somewhere. Once again, a superior song in the Stills' canon, although not quite matching the quality of the best songs on his debut album.

SUGAR BABE

Piano and organ dominate this song, in which Stills weaves an elaborate philosophical seduction. There's a didactic, machismo tone to the third verse in which he instructs his would-be partner on precisely how he should be treated. The final chorus includes the revealing line, "Come on sweet Rita you're my sugar babe", a fantasy assertion given the loss of Coolidge to partner Graham Nash. As if realizing this, he concedes, "Loving you from a distance never did make it anyway". Alas, the frustration that produced the song remains till the end as Stills offers himself false hope amid the self-ultimatum: "I got to get next to the girl or I got to get away".

KNOW YOU GOT TO RUN

Previously heard as the opening section to CSN&Y's 'Everybody I Love You', this was the original composition in its starker state, with Stills on banjo. Like most of the other songs on the album, the lyrics testify to Stills' complicated emotional interactions, a state of affairs that brings an element of fascination to the material under view.

OPEN SECRET

The closing track to the first half of the album is most notable for its bombastic brass as Stills rises to the occasion with some of his most portentous and extravagant lyrical exclamations. In a weird mix of vulnerability and unparalleled conceit he demands: "Someone tell me have I been gifted or robbed?" Even in emotional defeat, he inflates the nature of his art, proclaiming: "Will I sing my last symphony to an empty room?" Stills' vision of himself as a writer of grand symphonies rather than simple songs is exacerbated by the extraordinary brass interludes, more appropriate to a major motion picture soundtrack. This relatively fragile song, full of self-aggrandizing assertions, can barely support the epic brass crescendo, although Stills does attempt to chill out the track with a pleasant salsa refrain.

RELAXING TOWN

Testifying to his need to escape the rigours of the rock 'n' roll lifestyle, Stills imagines a more mundane existence. Casting his satirical eye over the current political scene he imagines a rally at Soldier's Field, featuring a battle royal between radical Jerry Rubin and the Major of Chicago, Richard Daley. "The American people have a few instincts that let's hope we can continue to use," he observed at the time. "A lot of people will rationalize that the Jerry Rubins are necessary and I don't buy it. What I saw awakened by Jerry Rubin, I don't want to see awakened."

SINGIN' CALL

This quiet acoustic ballad, notable for its rugged, pastoral imagery portrayed Stills as a pilgrim on a journey of spiritual fulfilment. He was sufficiently pleased with the song to revive it in later years on *Stills Alone*.

ECOLOGY SONG

The Memphis Horns reached their expansionist limits on this track, which included a full chorus backing Stills as he blasts forth his ecological pleas. More a rallying cry than a political solution, the overwhelming arrangement was unforgettable.

WORD GAME

Reverting to acoustic protest in Dylanesque mid-Sixties fashion, Stills offers some lyrically packed verses, with a sparse acoustic backing. His surly contempt is manifest in the final verse which culminates in the disgusted observation, "They might throw up on you". When performing the song on television or in concert, he would sometimes censor his own composition by substituting the words "throw up" with the coy "they might hear about you." Recalling the origins of the song, Stills explained: "When I was living in England in the early Seventies I saw a documentary about South Africa made by underground Black filmmakers. They shot it with hidden cameras, stuffed in a sack, or under a hat. It showed what it's really, really like to live under apartheid. It made me so mad that I wrote this song in about 15 minutes. The hard part was making it fit to music. When I began performing it live, I would often segue into 'Crossroads' and the two melted together. The real 'Crossroads' that is, not the rock 'n' roll version. The Robert Johnson version, rough and uneven, where he would have an 11-bar phrase, followed by a six-bar phrase, followed by seven bars. Before it became contrived. That's the type of situation 'Word Game' followed: it determined its own form based on how I held a word or turned a phrase during the performance."

MARIANNE

After the hard politics of 'Word Game' came this bland pop tune, which was subsequently issued as a single. Stills' unflattering falsetto vocal and the irksome refrain ensured that it was by far the weakest song on the album. Nevertheless, it reached number 42 in the US charts.

BLUEBIRD REVISITED

Originally performed with CSN&Y in concert, this would probably have appeared on *Déjà Vu* if Neil Young's contributions had not limited the number of songs available to Stills. With a strong organ backing, the Memphis Horns and a choir in full cry, Stills attempts an impossible reconciliation, punctuated by the despairing plea: "Come back home". He then seeks relief in the original 'Bluebird' which harks back to happier days in his relationship during the Buffalo Springfield period. There's also a conga break with a Latin tinge that is quite attractive and the expected brass crescendo. Although it is easy to tarnish Stills with accusations of self-indulgence as he lays his emotional life bare in increasingly melodramatic fashion, the exercise is not without its appeal. Like the bombastic 'Open Secret', the combination of ego unbound and deep hurt offers both an unintended comic pathos and cathartic release

graham nash
david crosby

CROSBY & NASH

GRAHAM NASH/DAVID CROSBY

ORIGINAL RELEASE DATE: APRIL 1972

The strong run of CSN&Y-related albums continued with this first duo album by Crosby & Nash. Both had enough strong songs to complete a set that was very impressive, with Crosby excelling himself courtesy of the stupendous pairing: 'Where Will I Be?'/'Page 43'. This album was preceded by a memorable series of acoustic concerts by Crosby & Nash that were unique in the annals of CSN&Y history. Although these were not the biggest or most lucrative dates played by the duo, they represented the true heart of their music – adventurous, intimate and emotionally charged. Their deconstruction of musical components in an attempt to unravel and capture the essence of a composition has seldom been bettered. An all-acoustic memento of those shows was released on the bootleg market under the title *A Very Stony Evening*. Back in the studio, the duo elected to flesh out the tracks with a select group of musical friends. The album proved another big chart success, reaching an impressive number 4 in the US charts.

SOUTHBOUND TRAIN

A folk-flavoured opening from Nash, with prominent harmonica, acoustic guitar and steel courtesy of Jerry Garcia. Nash's thoughtful lyrics were among the best he had ever written. "I was feeling very bad about the Vietnam War," he recalled. "I was feeling very bad about the way America was going. It seemed to me that out of the idealism of the Fifties and Sixties, it was turning to shit. And it was heading down. And I tried to find a metaphor for the country, and I realized that modern America was basically built on the railroads, on the exploration of the

West and bringing civilization with them, and then towns sprung up and the railroads were pushed a little further. So I used the train as a metaphor for America, and it's going south. That's why it's called the Southbound train." After playing a show in New York, Crosby & Nash had an informal meeting with Bob Dylan back at their hotel. The master asked them about their latest material and they played him this song. "Sing it again," he insisted, much to the pride of Nash, who dined out on that story many times.

WHOLE CLOTH

Crosby's love of unexpected time signatures and rhythm shifts was evident on this track, which featured strong backing from Russ Kunkel (drums), Leland Sklar (bass), Craig Doerge (piano), and some noteworthy solos by lead guitarist Danny 'Kootch' Kortchmar. The song reaches a froth of righteous indignation in the final verse when Crosby expresses his anger after reading news reports questioning the sincerity of counter-culture musicians.

BLACKNOTES

Recorded live at Carnegie Hall when Nash was awaiting the arrival of Crosby and Stills on stage, this 58-second piano lesson later became a familiar part of Graham and David's concerts as an acoustic duo. Few would have expected this piece of pensive stage humour to appear on an album, where its charm was decidedly ephemeral.

STRANGER'S ROOM

Originally written in 1969 and completed at the Chateau Marmont, this was another of Nash's darker, more reflective songs. The musical backing by the Section is particularly impressive and just for variety three French horn players are among the guest musicians. The inspiration for the song was Joni Mitchell whom Nash was desperately trying to forget when he awoke in another woman's house.

WHERE WILL I BE?

Crosby has seldom been better than this. Exquisite acoustic guitar playing, chillingly powerful vocals and some of the most despairing lyrics he has ever penned, characterized this work which equalled the majesty of his best work on the brilliant *If I Could Only Remember My Name*. Dana Africa plays flute on the track which reaches a disconcerting, awe-inspiring conclusion, punctuated by the words: "You tell me what am I going to do?"

PAGE 43

The answer song to 'Where Will I Be?', this *carpe diem* acceptance of life was the first sign of Crosby's recovery following his depression after the death of girlfriend Christine Hinton. Beautifully sung, with a sumptuous melody this, along with its predecessor, took the album to new heights of quality. Appropriately, Crosby completed this composition during a therapeutic period in which he sailed extensively. "I wrote it

in the main cabin of my boat in Sausalito," he remembered. "It was under the influence musically of James Taylor. I had been listening to how many passing chords he used... so the next song that I started writing I was fooling around with a set of changes that was like that, and that's what came."

FROZEN SMILES

With Nash back on harmonica, this seemed a passing protest song at some unnamed individual. Yet, it contained some of Nash's most bitter lines: "And if you carry on the way you did today/All the music in my veins will turn to stone". Nash later revealed that the subject of the song was none other than Stephen Stills. That knowledge adds a new dimension to the composition, providing a real eye-opener to the fractured ongoing CSN&Y relationship.

GAMES

Written in 1968, not long after he was fired by the Byrds, this was another very strong song from Crosby whose work during this period was exceptional. Here, he confronts the ramifications of his own ego, set against an enticing melody and a strong, committed vocal.

GIRL TO BE ON MY MIND

On 31 December 1970, Nash saw in the New Year at his San Francisco home, tinkering on a Wurlitzer piano and composing this song. Given his romantic adventures, it's hard to picture Nash worrying about finding the right girlfriend, although being alone on New Year's Eve no doubt made him feel sorry for himself. Although not a bad song, its style and mood, complete with church organ, did not fit well with the other material on this album.

THE WALL SONG

Originally written several years before, this was another opportunity for Crosby to play alongside Grateful Dead members, Jerry Garcia and Phil Lesh. The song features some of Crosby's most thoughtful lyrics, with a theme reminiscent of 'Mind Gardens', although without the dissonance of that controversial cut.

IMMIGRATION MAN

This closing track featured Nash at his most sarcastic, with all the exuberant harmonic attack of the Hollies. Undoubtedly, one of his best and most familiar of the time, it was based on a true incident. After playing a show in Vancouver, Nash was shocked to find himself temporarily barred entry back into the USA. As he explained: "Coming back across the border, Neil got in, David got in, Stephen got in, but I didn't because I was on an H-1 visa at the time from England. I was not an American citizen and they weren't going to let me in. In the meantime, there were people asking me for my autograph, you know? I showed that I had money and credit cards, that I'd only come across to work and was going back. And he wouldn't let me in. It pissed me off very badly. I took a cab to my house, and sat down immediately at the piano. And I wrote 'Immigration Man' on the back of a book called *The Silver Locust* by Ray Bradbury. It was the first thing that I could find." Nash's ability to pen commercial material, with strong hooklines, was seldom better exemplified than on this recording. In order to bolster the track, he added Dave Mason on lead guitar, with Greg Reeves (bass) and Johnny Barbata (drums). However, it says much for the appeal of the song that it was equally good, and arguably even better, when Nash played it alone with a thumping piano backing.

MANASSAS

MANASSAS

ORIGINAL RELEASE DATE: APRIL 1972

Even during the golden period of CSN&Y, the emergence of Manassas was something special. Those fortunate enough to have witnessed their live performances still speak with reverential enthusiasm about the power of their concerts. Still at his ambitious best, Stills assembled a crack team of musicians comprising Chris Hillman (vocals/guitar/mandolin), Al Perkins (vocals/steel guitar/guitar), Joe Lala (vocals/congas/timbale/percussion), Dallas Taylor (drums), Paul Harris (organ/ piano)/clavinette) and Calvin "Fuzzy" Samuels (bass). Their talents could barely be contained within the context of a single album, so Stills elected to record a double set. It says much for his songwriting skills at the time that there was little or no filler on the album. Truly, this was one of the few indispensable double albums to be recorded during the early Seventies. An extraordinarily eclectic collection, even by Stills' standards, it split neatly into four sides titled "The Raven", "The Wilderness", "Consider" and "Rock 'n' Roll Is Here To Stay". For the man nicknamed Captain Manyhands, this was the ultimate musical excursion, bookending a remarkable run of release stretching back to his Buffalo Springfield days. Although the album reached number 4 in the US charts and augured well commercially, Manassas was to prove an all too brief and much missed chapter in Stills' recording life. Chris Hillman's memory of this record was in accord with the general view of the work. "I like the whole album," he told me. "A lot of people have said it should have been a single album, but I think it's a great double. And it's very rare for me to come from a project and say, 'That's wonderful'. Manassas had really good players in it. It had the capacity to do anything from bluegrass to Latin. It was rewarding. I learned a lot, and it was very stimulating for the period it lasted."

SONG OF LOVE

Subtitling the first quarter of the album The Raven suggested that we were about to receive a series of meditations on Stills' doomed relationship with Rita Coolidge. In fact, the lyrics were much more oblique than expected and generally subservient to the instrumentation. One of the highlights of this opening track was Al Perkins' fine steel guitar playing and Joe Lala's inventive percussion. Stills' wah-wah guitar work provided the song with its keen edge.

JET SET (SIGH)

'Song Of Love' segues directly into this track, which is split into two movements. An insistent riff, reinforced by the blues harmonica of Sydney George, heralds Stills' warnings about the dangers of being a rock 'n' roll star, after which the song moves into a fascinating fusion titled "cuban bluegrass". Backed by Lala, Stills rediscovers his Latin youth and tags on an energetic ending redolent of the closing part of 'Suite: Judy Blue Eyes'. As Stills enthused: "The clincher came when we recorded 'Jet Set', which was one of the first things we did. When I was a kid learning how to play, older musicians used to throw a riff at me and see if they could lose me... They'd see if you were on your toes by trying to lose you. Anyway, just for fun, I threw a gut-bucket blues at Al Perkins, who was a friend of Chris's and I didn't know him all that well at the time. Well, he knocked me down, he was so good. And that's when I decided that this could be a band – that was the clincher."

ANYWAY

Another great interchange of instruments with Manassas fully demonstrating their versatility as players. Stills and Lala share vocals, which adds another dimension to the sound.

BOTH OF US (BOUND TO LOSE)

Chris Hillman co-wrote this track on which he provides the opening vocal and trades off successive lines with Stills. The lyrics conclude with Stills' resonant question: "Is that really how you see me, just a statue making sounds?" Even the great musical explorers are eventually depersonalized to become merely joint statues for spectators to admire. Two years later, Neil Young presented a comparable image in 'For The Turnstiles' in which "All the great explorers are now in granite laid" awaiting their unveiling. There, the artist, transmuted into a statue, becomes merely something to be looked at. Stills could have ended his composition with a similarly bleak image but instead shifted the tempo and entire mood of the piece by concluding with a Latin/salsa flourish, which featured one of his great rhythmic solos.

FALLEN EAGLE

The second section of the album, subtitled The Wilderness, was devoted entirely to country music. Stills' sardonic observations on the plight of the eagle were given even greater momentum by the rousing mandolin work of Hillman and the introduction of world champion fiddle player Byron Berline.

JESUS GAVE LOVE AWAY FOR FREE

Paul Harris's honky-tonk piano dominates Stills' urbane reflection on monogamy and a mysterious dark-haired lady. The title of the song is not revealed until the final line of the last verse.

COLORADO

Hillman's last studio album prior to joining Manassas was *The Flying Burrito Brothers*, the highlight of which was a beautiful ballad from Rick Roberts titled 'Colorado'. Coincidentally, Stills came up with a song of the same title and theme. The dark lady of the previous track appears once again as Stills contrasts urban and pastoral ways of life.

SO BEGINS THE TASK

This was arguably the closest that Stills reached to writing a potential standard. A beautiful melody was complemented by some of Stills' most poignant lyrics, which even made good dramatic use of his legendary insomnia. Al Perkins excels himself on pedal steel, while Stills enacts the torture of adjusting to a changed relationship. From bitterness to acceptance, he finally finds some salvation in the knowledge that even in loss there is growth. The song was covered extremely well by Judy Collins, who was most likely the subject of Stills' angst.

Written long before this album was released, the song had been played at many of the early CSN&Y shows. It was amazing that Stills waited so long to record this classic which could have graced the first CS&N album, *Déjà Vu* or his solo album. "I thought of this song as a poem," he concluded. "It was written immediately after 'Helplessly Hoping'. It's a song of loss but also the freedom that goes with loss. It was conceived of as an acoustic song."

HIDE IT SO DEEP

One of the most pronounced country songs on the album, this featured strong work by Berline on fiddle, Hillman on mandolin and Harris on keyboards. Stills' country phrasing is particularly notable.

DON'T LOOK AT MY SHADOW

Stills' country travelogue details his performing history from a brash youth in Texas through to exploits in New Orleans, New York, bayou country and finally a memorable gig at LA Forum before 20,000 fans. As the pace quickens, Stills explains how he was almost outdone by the rock 'n' roll lifestyle ("California dreaming nearly put me down for good") before finding solace in his new home ("Colorado rocky mountains saved my senses"). Berline and company bring the song to a suitably exuberant close.

IT DOESN'T MATTER

The original version of this song was written by Stills, Hillman and Rick Roberts, but did not appear until as late as 1976 on the first Firefall album. Roberts' words were excised from the Manassas cut which remains the definitive reading. The melody was again very strong with some great vocal interchanges between Stills and Hillman. "I felt the song 'It Doesn't Matter' captured a lot of that Buffalo Springfield sound," Hillman noted. "There's a certain moment near the end of the song where there's a track-layered harmony and Stephen is doing a guitar figure which sounds like a bass. It's very rhythmic and it really makes the last chorus great; it boosts the track with something subtle and completely out of context. I really had to stand up on my toes to play with these guys and I needed to be challenged at that point in my life. He made me try harder."

JOHNNY'S GARDEN

One of Stills' most beguiling vocals and subtle tributes, this song was inspired by the gardener who worked at Brookfield House in Elstead, Surrey. Stills had purchased the estate from Ringo Starr, the previous owner being actor Peter Sellers. The gardener was the one constant whose love for the estate was manifested in the perfectly kept grounds. "He had soul," Stills enthused. "He was a herbalist and used to make incredible herbal teas. The song was written at a time in my life when I was on the road constantly and what I really needed was to stay at home and tend my garden." Stills portrays the garden as his refuge from the exigencies of the rock business, but he is quick to realize that it is his money that has bought this privilege. Downplaying pastoral sentimentality, he quips: "Only trouble was I had to buy it."

BOUND TO FALL

Another strong melody with some intriguing harmony work, this Mike Brewer composition was brought to the group by Chris Hillman

who had previously cut the song as an outtake during the sessions for *The Notorious Byrd Brothers* in 1967. Brewer & Shipley later recorded their own version.

HOW FAR

This mid-paced number again revealed Stills attempting to reconcile his conflicting feelings about platonic love and unrequited passion, themes that dominated his work for much of this period.

MOVE AROUND

Here Stills gets philosophical, pondering the question, "What do we do given life?" Like a biologist, he concludes, "We move around". Playing a Moog synthesizer programmed by Malcolm Cecil, Stills creates some interesting effects. There is a sudden change of tempo before the final verse in which he presents some of his most abstruse but intriguing lyrical conceits. Eschewing his usually straightforward lines, he proclaims: "The acceptance of error with grace is to refuse to be vain and so afraid of losing face this fear drives one further into what one thinks to be a race of life... or death." Heavy.

THE LOVE GANGSTER

Stills again plays some exceptional guitar breaks on this blues original co-written by Rolling Stone Bill Wyman, who also plays bass on the track. Wyman was so enamoured of Manassas that he allegedly considered leaving the Stones to join them, although I suspect that was simply a rhetorical gesture. In the final verse to this song, Stills describes the omnipresence of the police, recalling the theme of his Buffalo Springfield classic, 'For What It's Worth'.

WHAT TO DO

The final section of the album is titled "Rock 'n' Roll Is Here To Stay". However, the opening track is almost vaudevillian in its execution. There were some strange goings-on during the chorus leading into the line "Blind stubborn pride drove us apart". As Stills explained: "There's this little box and Dallas (Taylor) twisted that knob and Ronnie (Albert) twisted the other one on a different box and I left the room because I didn't like what I played anyway, and waited for the next verse with the tack piano in it, which I do like. So much, in fact, that I ran back into the room and dove into the speakers only to return again disguised as a bus driver who directed the next chorus." Byron Berline ended the track with a flourish that Stills described as "an outtasite fiddle solo", adding, "Byron is too good a fiddler to be hampered by little knobs and crazy people in the studio."

RIGHT NOW

A favourite live track, which features another excellent vocal interchange between Stills and Hillman. At the start of the second verse, Stills changes the words from "who was it cast the mould" to "who was it froze", before describing a girl he once knew, concluding, "One of my best friends took her down with his games for sure". Although no names are mentioned, the suspicion remains that he is singing about Rita Coolidge and Graham Nash. There's some strong guitar soloing by Stills enhanced by the careful piano playing of Paul Harris. By the end of the song, Stills rejects past and future and determines to settle in "the right now".

THE TREASURE

At eight minutes in length, this was the album's magnum opus. What should have been one of the most exciting and show-stopping numbers in Manassas' arsenal was partially spoiled by a strangely muddy mix and a production that lacked clarity. The track could and should have been so much sharper and crisper, but it's still a great number in which Stills relates his romantic travails, while playing some spectacular wah-wah guitar. Mid-way through, he breaks loose for a stunning solo backed by the full power of Manassas. It's a real tour de force and a fitting penultimate conclusion to the album.

BLUES MAN

Signing off with a requiem for Jimi The Fox (Hendrix), The Owl (Al Wilson) and Skydog (Duane Allman), Stills offers a heartfelt acoustic blues tribute to "Three good men I knew well/Never see again".

STEPHEN STILLS

MANASSAS

CHRIS HILLMAN
JOE LALA
AL PERKINS

DALLAS TAYLOR
FUZZY SAMUEL
PAUL HARRIS

DOWN THE ROAD

MANASSAS

DOWN THE ROAD

ORIGINAL RELEASE DATE: APRIL 1973

Manassas' second album was a frustratingly patchy affair and inevitably anti-climactic in the wake of its great predecessor. Although there were several high points on the album, it was difficult to avoid the conclusion that some of Manassas' edge had been blunted. Confusion and indecision surrounded the recording and there was disagreement over the choice of material. "That second album is a story in itself," Hillman told me with a rueful sigh. "It originally had all this material that was subsequently deleted. There was even a song that Fuzzy, Dallas, Al and Joe wrote called 'Mama Told Me So'. Then Ahmet Ertegun came down and wanted to put more of Stephen's songs on it. Thus, there are those tunes such as 'City Junkies', which I don't really care for. That second album wasn't good." Certainly, there were some strange decisions, most notably the deletion of one of Stills' better lyrics and melodies, 'Thoroughfare Gap', which would not surface on record for the best part of seven years. Other omissions included 'High And Dry', 'White Nigger' (originally recorded with Jimi Hendrix) and 'Witching Hour' (which Hillman later recorded for his first solo album). For all its occasional shortcomings, few would part with the album's greatest moments, which left a longing for more Manassas material in the future. Sadly, it was not to be. The sheer size of the group ensured that they would never reconvene in a belated reunion project but instead leave behind fond memories of some of the best live music of the era.

ISN'T IT ABOUT TIME

The album opens with a Stills protest song, punctuated by some striking slide guitar. An insistent, compelling riff works well, with Paul Harris's piano rising in the mix at crucial moments.

LIES

Solely written by Chris Hillman, this track revealed a musical debt to the Rolling Stones. An average but catchy song with a tinge of misogyny reminiscent of The Flying Burrito Brothers' 'Christine's Tune', it is largely salvaged by Hillman's surly vocal and Manassas' usually strong instrumentation.

PENSAMIENTO

Surely the highlight of the album, this collaboration between Stills and Nelson Escoto was written and sung entirely in Spanish. It remains the most pure and convincing example of Stills' Latin excursions. A flute solo by Stills' friend Sydney George is perfectly placed, taking the song to a much higher level than most of the material on this album.

SO MANY TIMES

Further proof of Manassas' eclecticism is provided by the sudden switch from Latin to country. Hillman's mandolin introduces this superior collaboration with Stills, which includes some portentous lyrics and a fine steel guitar solo by Al Perkins.

BUSINESS ON THE STREET

Stills attempts to resolve the art/commerce dichotomy, in this amusingly infectious but decidedly average cut. The playing and singing is looser than usual. "Some of the vocals and things should have been done over," Stills admitted, "but I was lazy."

DO YOU REMEMBER THE AMERICANS

With Stills on banjo, this is bluegrass Manassas style. The problems of a longhair hitching a lift encourages Stills to speculate flippantly on veterans returning from the war and the changing attitude of the American people.

DOWN THE ROAD

The title track was another blues lament, with Stills playing the black soulman, complete with phrases such as "Chirren" instead of children. P. P. Arnold was recruited as backing vocalist to add some soul to the proceedings. The song was most notable for the arrogance of the fifth verse in which Stills speculates on Jesus and Zen before concluding: "I'm just into everyday, I don't hide from where I've been".

CITY JUNKIES

Evidence of imagination failing was evident here as Stills opened a second consecutive song with the line: "When I was a young man". The piano introduction and accompanying arrangement sound straight out of The Rolling Stones' 'Let's Spend The Night Together'. This was one of the tracks added to the album at a later date, much to the disappointment of Chris Hillman.

GUAGUANCO DE VERO

Stills teamed up with Joe Lala for this catchy reflection on his troubled emotional past and new-found happiness in the arms of French singer Veronique Sanson. Stills had met her in Paris during a Manassas tour and they subsequently married in March 1973.

ROLLIN' MY STONE

Bassist Calvin "Fuzzy" Samuels enjoyed a rare writing collaboration with Stills on this decidedly dull finale to the album. Stills was previously known for beginning and ending albums on a strong note but, on this occasion, he allowed the work to fizzle out in lacklustre fashion.

GRAHAM NASH
WILD TALES

GRAHAM NASH

WILD TALES

ORIGINAL RELEASE DATE: JANUARY 1974

There may have been more famous and individually impressive songs on Nash's first solo album, but this was arguably more cohesive as a mood piece. Unusually understated, even by Nash's standards, it was a lot less self-conscious lyrically, and all the better for it. Whereas his previous work had shown a tendency towards a cloying sentimentality and an ego couched in a sometimes self-deluded humility, this more neatly balanced the personal and the social, with Nash looking outwards. As a result the starker tones rang truer. Probably the most underrated of his albums, this deserves closer attention.

WILD TALES

Nash's electric rhythm guitar fuses perfectly with David Lindley's electric slide to provide a strong backing track for this highly-amusing tale which, incredibly, was based on an actual event. "A friend of Elliot Roberts had this incredible series of mishaps all in one week," Nash recalled. "His house was flooded, all his possessions were destroyed, and to top it off his old lady ran away with the milkman. He even went as far as to hire a detective to film her making love to the milkman. When her lawyer came to ask for alimony, his lawyer showed the film. Wild tales from the East."

HEY YOU (LOOKING AT THE MOON)

Ben Keith plays steel guitar as Nash goes country on this easy-going track. The style doesn't really suit Nash although, with Stills' assistance, he had previously pulled off a successful country arrangement with 'Teach Your Children'.

PRISON SONG

Undoubtedly one of the best Nash songs of the period, this song fused autobiography with reflections on institutionalized injustice. Nash recollects a key childhood incident when his father was arrested after being found in possession of a stolen camera. As a result of refusing to grass on a colleague, Nash Snr faced the full weight of legal wrath and was sentenced to a year's imprisonment. "It really broke him and he died shortly afterwards," Nash recalled. The second verse was inspired by a letter Nash received from a kid in Texas who was serving a staggering 10-year stretch for possession of marijuana. In the song, Nash contrasts his fate with another man's five dollar fine for a similar offence in Ann Arbor, Michigan. Nash's commitment to prison reform was further demonstrated via the concerts that he and Crosby undertook at various correctional facilities.

YOU'LL NEVER BE THE SAME

With Ben Keith back on steel guitar, this was a second attempt to complement the mood of the work with a country number. Unfortunately, the song lacked the strength of the other material on the album.

AND SO IT GOES

A successful mood piece by Nash, with Neil Young on piano and Crosby helping with the harmonic blend. Although resigned and reflective, Nash resists slipping into maudlin self-indulgence.

GRAVE CONCERN

Nash's ominous lyrics, complete with meteorological analogies, were a highlight of this song documenting America's social malaise in the mid-Seventies. The jaunty rhythm, with Lindley's electric slide prominent, gave the track an edge, while Stanley Johnson's use of a voice montage worked well. Easily one of the best tracks on the album, this was subsequently a key song on CSN&Y's famous 1974 tour.

OH! CAMIL (THE WINTER SOLDIER)

With Nash on acoustic guitar, harmonica and

vocals, this was written in the protest song style of early/mid-Sixties Bob Dylan. Its vibrant and graphic anti-war message later brought Nash some unexpected friction at a 1988 Vietnam Veterans' benefit in Boston. "There were six Vets in the audience and they didn't like me singing that song because it was such a negative perspective of the Vets," Nash recalled. "When Scott Camil told me his story he told me about killing all these people and making piles of bodies and standing on them, taking photographs. And when I wrote about that, what I was talking about was how much war affects human beings. I guess it upset a few Vets...".

I MISS YOU

With Nash on piano/vocals assisted by bassist Tim Drummond, this stark ballad was quite effective. By using understatement and simple observation in place of self-conscious concentration on his own pain, Nash produced a much more effective account of romantic loss.

ON THE LINE

A pretty melody and by far the best of the three country-influenced numbers on the album, this arch reflection on the price of stardom was a pleasant diversion. Crosby makes a guest appearance on backing vocals, though his presence is hardly noticeable.

ANOTHER SLEEP SONG

Arguably the highlight of the entire album, this beautifully constructed ballad easily outclassed the previous 'Sleep Song' on *Songs For Beginners*. After instructing Joel Bernstein on acoustic guitar, Nash lays down a lingering melody, enhanced by Ben Keith on dobro. Best of all is the bewitching closing harmony by Joni Mitchell, matching the sound of the dobro and providing a fragile but resounding conclusion to the album. Explaining the origin of this second sleep song, Nash recalled: "This was written in Barbra Streisand's living room on her piano while she sat on a sofa eating a TV dinner. How many people hate to get out of bed in the morning, hate to face the world? You don't want to answer the phone or talk to anybody. Well, me too, except that all we need is someone to awaken us. That's what we need, that's what the song is about."

Stereo
CBS
69146

Stills

STEPHEN STILLS

STILLS

ORIGINAL RELEASE DATE: JUNE 1975

For his first album with CBS, Stills offered some of his most impressive compositions of recent years, producing what many would argue was his last great solo album. Over 20 years on, it still sounds like an unrecognized classic of its period, released at a time when we were truly spoiled by quality material from CSN&Y in all their permutations. Stills later went through very lazy periods as a songwriter, but here the material was extremely focused. Most of the songs are positive and uplifting without ever lapsing into saccharine sweetness. A notable achievement that deserved far greater commercial success.

TURN BACK THE PAGES

Co-written by Stills and Donnie Dacus, with Marcie Levy on backing vocals, this was recorded late in the sessions at Criteria by the Albert Brothers. The perfect opening track, it was Stills at his sparkling best, with a commercial song and upfront production.

MY FAVORITE CHANGES

Despite the title, the melody sounded anything but hackneyed, while the expressive lyrics, detailing Veronique Sanson's pregnancy and Stills' new-found maturity, were impressive. The backing track featuring Stills, Dacus, Leland Sklar and Joe Lala, was cut in Sausalito. At a later date in Colorado, Stills added vocals, with assistance from Kenny Passarelli and Peggy Clinger.

MY ANGEL

This was an older song, which Stills had completed after jamming with Dallas Taylor. Joe Lala added some percussion and Stills himself played bass, piano, clavinet and organ. The high quality of the song indicated Stills' determination to record absolutely top notch material for his new record company, CBS.

IN THE WAY

Another strong song, characterized by tight harmonies and some memorable guitar work. This fitted perfectly with the mood of the album, underlining Stills' ability to sequence the tracks and choose the right material.

LOVE STORY

One of Stills' most remarkable lyrics, this was written four years previously during what must now be seen as a golden age of singer-songwriter creativity. The song's ending, so subtle and impressive, featured Stills at his most lyrical. At one point, he intended to use strings to add some atmosphere to the track, but finally decided that the song worked better in its stark state. The vocals were among the best that Stills has recorded and took over 20 hours to complete.

TO MAMA FROM CHRISTOPHER AND THE OLD MAN

This exuberant song about Stills' relationship with his son, and how it strengthened the emotional bond between himself and his wife Veronique Sanson, is a charming piece. The song was written and recorded within a 24-hour cycle. Stills recalls returning home at 7 am after a session, playing with his son who had just awoken, then returning to the studio inspired. Speaking of himself in the third person, he noted: "Cut the basis, bass and second rhythm, then Tubby (Ziegler) overdubbed the drums, with Stills hanging over his shoulder with a tambourine. We got smoking and did it in eight hours, including mixdown."

FIRST THINGS FIRST

Co-written by Stills, Joe Schermie and Jon Smith, this heavily percussive track, featuring Dallas Taylor and Joe Lala, was another extremely solid work, with Crosby, Nash and Kenny Passarelli on backing vocals.

NEW MAMA

Stills' reading of Neil Young's song of new parenthood, was a much slicker version than the original on *Tonight's The Night*. It's a good cover, however, with a theme that complements several of the other songs of new-born optimism.

AS I COME OF AGE

This was originally recorded in London back in 1971 with Stills on piano and Ringo Starr on drums. Stills later overdubbed organ and bass, Donnie Dacus provided the lead guitar, and Crosby & Nash were commandeered for the backing vocals. Once again, the lyrics were a reflection on Stills's transition into a second stage of manhood and maturity at the age of 26.

SHUFFLE JUST AS BAD

That a song as impressive as this was probably the weakest track on the album is comment enough on the exceptional quality of the record. With Russ Kunkel on drums, Jerry Aeillo on piano and Stills playing the remaining instruments, they fashioned a neat blues riff with the shuffle at the end sounding especially good.

COLD COLD WORLD

Co-written by Stills and Donnie Dacus, this was another of the Criteria tracks recorded by the Albert Brothers. Another candidate for best album track, it included some spinetingling wah-wah guitar interchanges between Stills and Dacus, with drummer Conrad Isidore and percussionist Joe Lala providing an irresistible rhythm. The soulful vocals were given an extra bite courtesy of Betty White.

MYTH OF SISYPHUS

This was a one take song with Stills on piano/vocals, assisted by drummer Jimmy Fox. Claudia Lanier was later recruited to beef up the backing vocal. Premiered on CSN&Y's 1974 tour, this was one of Stills' most eagerly-awaited songs, with intelligent lyrics, directed at his evolving relationship with Veronique Sanson. A thoughtful conclusion to a highly impressive album.

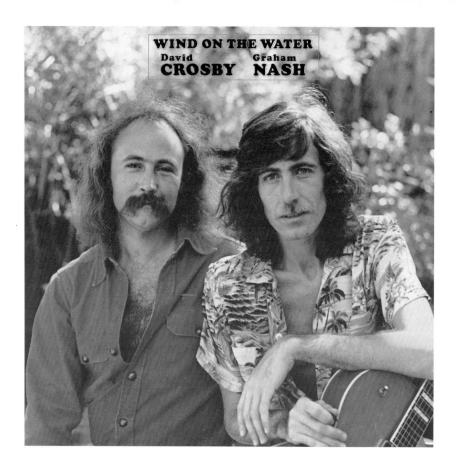

WIND ON THE WATER
David **CROSBY** Graham **NASH**

CROSBY & NASH

WIND ON THE WATER

ORIGINAL RELEASE DATE: SEPTEMBER 1975

After Crosby, Stills, Nash & Young failed to complete a studio album, following their immensely successful stadium tour of 1974, the participants drifted into solo projects. Weary of the ongoing problems with the CSN&Y circus, Crosby & Nash decided to re-estab-lish their career as a duo in the most emphatic way possible. As Nash explained: "Having spent many thousands of dollars on tape with CSN&Y, we did an about turn and decided to concentrate on me and David, and not worry about it. Let the past go... CSN&Y is a very mag-ical thing to me – something very precious – and the tendency to want it to materialize can stop you in your forward motion a lot of times. Frankly, we were getting sick of that happening and decided to forget it." With fresh management and a new label, they completed a sterling selection of songs for a release that remains their most accomplished as a duo. Other C&N albums had individually strong songs, but this one was consistently excellent from beginning to end. The musicianship from the Section was exemplary and it came as no surprise when they joined C&N for a critically-acclaimed tour soon after this release. Fortunately, Crosby & Nash's exemplary songwriting was rewarded with chart success as the album climbed to number 6 in the US, their best ever showing as a duo. This album remains Crosby & Nash at their most highly recommended.

CARRY ME

As Crosby himself stresses, this is one of the greatest songs he ever wrote. Its alluring melody, reinforced by Crosby's fine 6 and 12 string electric guitar and James Taylor's acoustic accompaniment, provides a perfect backdrop to the elegiac reflections on friends and family now lost. The second verse may be about the deceased Christine Hinton or, if not, an earlier girlfriend. The themes of both 'Why' and 'Triad' are reiterated in the references to parental repression, a favourite subject of Crosby's. In the third verse, Crosby recalls his mother wasting away from cancer, yet finding hope even in the face of impending death. As Crosby remembers, her condition encouraged him to consider euthanasia. "She was lying in hospital, dying of cancer, and wanted to go while she still had some dignity," he remembers. "She asked me to do it, set her free... I said, 'Hell, yes'. I learned how to do it from a doctor friend and I was perfectly willing to do it. I'm not ashamed to say that. But she found out if she didn't die in hospital and on a doctor's schedule, they'd conduct an autopsy and charge me with murder."

MAMA LION

Another interesting arrangement, with Crosby, Nash and Danny Kootch (Kortchmar) playing electric guitars, and David Lindley adding some arresting slide guitar. The track has real body, the melody is insistent and the lyrics intriguing. Although the identity of Nash's 'Mama Lion' is conjectural, the smart money indicates that it is Joni Mitchell.

BITTERSWEET

Written by Crosby in the Chateau Marmont on Sunset Boulevard on Nash's Wurlitzer piano, this was recorded within a day of its composition. "We've always tried to find the shortest route from our minds on to the tape," Crosby insisted. "It's a song about duality". Again, the song is of high quality with Carole King on electric organ and Craig Doerge on electric piano.

TAKE THE MONEY AND RUN

The formidable fiddle and electric slide playing of David Lindley added depth to Nash's oblique comment on rock star avarice. His urgent vocal and sarcastic tone perhaps summed up a period of transition for Crosby & Nash. The year before they had partaken in massive money-making stadium tours with CSN&Y, then parted with manager Elliot Roberts and changed labels from Atlantic to ABC/Polydor.

NAKED IN THE RAIN

This was the only Crosby/Nash writing collaboration on the album. Once more, the songwriting is top notch and this track features some of the best C&N harmonies on the record. Nash adds some congas which complement the understated feel of the track.

LOVE WORK OUT

Nash's insistent piano work and Craig Doerge's background organ playing set the scene for this unusual song on the nature of relationships. Ostensibly, a karmic love song there is also an underlying, more cynical sense of love as a commercial transaction. Nash is in passionate voice throughout and David Lindley provides a sinewy solo, with Crosby and Kootch adding further bite on guitar.

LOW DOWN PAYMENT

As well as Doerge's electric and acoustic piano work, there is a treble electric guitar assault from Crosby, Nash and Kootch, which beefs up this fascinating track. The

rhythm work is most impressive with Crosby incorporating different time signatures to dramatic effect. With Lindley also offering some scintillating slide work, the result is nothing less than one of the best tracks on the record. The song remains a largely unheralded gem in the Crosby catalogue.

COWBOY OF DREAMS

Nash transforms himself into a honky tonk country singer for this amusing pastoral excursion. There's a sly reference to Crosby in the line: "I took a look at the hole where the Byrd used to be". However, the cowboy of the title was actually Neil Young, whose eccentricities were documented in the allusion: "I heard that the house and the barn had a blend". Recalling the incident, Nash explained: "I once went down to his ranch and he rowed me out into the middle of the lake – putting my life in his hands once again. He waved at someone invisible and music started to play, in the countryside. I realized Neil had his house wired as the left speaker, and his barn as the right speaker. And Elliot Mazer, his engineer, said, 'How is it?' And Neil shouted back, 'More barn!'"

HOMEWARD THROUGH THE HAZE

The only song of Crosby's to mention Samson Agonistes, this maintained the consistently high quality of David's other songs on the album. Russ Kunkel's drumming deserves special commendation, while the combined vocal power of Crosby, Nash and Carole King is exhilarating. King's guest appearance on this album was a reciprocal thank-you to Crosby & Nash for their contributions to her recent work, Thoroughbred.

FIELDWORKER

This powerful commentary on migrant worker exploitation momentarily transformed Nash into a modern-day Woody Guthrie. Like 'Deportee', 'Fieldworker' eloquently portrayed the casual disregard for the easily exploited. Nash's complaint was given greater emphasis by the sustained steel guitar work of Ben Keith and David Lindley, while the additional musicians included pianist Stan Szeleat and The Band's Levon Helm.

TO THE LAST WHALE...
A. CRITICAL MASS,
B. WIND ON THE WATER

Crosby's wordless mantra 'Critical Mass' was arguably the best chant progression that he ever wrote or recorded. Along with 'Song With No Words (Tree With No Leaves)' and 'I'd Swear There Was Somebody Here', this was Crosby at his most brilliant. The chant serves as a requiem, setting the scene for Nash's partly elegiac 'Wind On The Water', a persuasive and moving ecological lament on the plight of whales. With unintended humour, Nash, in conversation with *Song Talk*'s Paul Zollo, suggested that the fate of whales was linked in his mind with public reaction to his partner David Crosby. Recalling how the Byrds were "harpooned" by critics on their 1965 visit to England, Nash concluded: "People have always been throwing harpoons at Crosby. Always. Some of them stick, some of them don't. So, as a matter of fact, even though it is a song that evolved into a statement about how we treat the Great Whales, and that great statement of Gandhi's that the signpost of every civilization is how it treats its pets and its animals, it really started with two magazines in the back of my car, and my thoughts about David."

STEPHEN STILLS LIVE

ELECTRIC SIDE: WOODEN SHIPS/FOUR DAYS GONE
JET SET (SIGH)/ROCKY MOUNTAIN WAY/SPECIAL CARE

STEPHEN STILLS

STEPHEN STILLS LIVE

ORIGINAL RELEASE DATE: DECEMBER 1975

Recorded 8/9 March 1974 at the Auditorium Theatre, Chicago, this live album preceded the re-emergence of CSN&Y later in the year. Essentially a snapshot of Stills at a not particularly exciting or innovative period in his performing career, it included an acoustic reading of Fred Neil's 'Everybody's Talkin', a blues excursion combining 'Crossroads' and 'You Can't Catch Me', a less intense 'Word Game', an electric version of 'Wooden Ships' on which Crosby was sorely missed, a surprise reprise of a couple of old Buffalo Springfield tunes ('Four Days Gone' and 'Special Care') and a stodgy medley of 'Jet Set (Sigh)' and 'Rocky Mountain Way'. By the time of the album's release at the end of 1975, it seemed completely redundant as a document of Stills' performing work and only served to remind listeners that the much superior CSN&Y reunion concerts had failed to produce a live album. Others mourned the fact that something as dull as this existed in preference to a Manassas live album, which would have been much more appetizing.

Full track listing: Electric side: Wooden Ships; Four Days Gone; Jet Set (Sigh)/Rocky Mountain Way; Special Care; Acoustic side: Change Partners; Crossroads/You Can't Catch Me; Everybody's Talkin' (At Me); 4+20; Word Game.

STEPHEN STILLS
ILLEGAL STILLS
ORIGINAL RELEASE DATE: MAY 1976

Stills' studio work had been exemplary up until this release but suddenly everything went wrong. The album lacked invention or imagination, the general quality of the songs was weak and the decision to allow Stills' protégé Donnie Dacus a share of the vocals only made matters worse. For the first time, Stills looked as though he was resting on his laurels and his seemingly effortless songwriting skills had clearly deserted him, resulting in an unusually lacklustre and formulaic record. It still sold moderately well, peaking at number 31 in the US charts.

BUYIN' TIME
Middlingly pleasant, this was ultimately a failed attempt to rekindle the effervescent power of 'Love The One You're With'. Written in the midst of the 1975 Presidential placations over economic problems, it brought out the pessimist in Stills: "America the dream is lost and it's killing me and you".

MIDNIGHT IN PARIS
Co-written by Veronique Sanson and Donnie Dacus, this song featured Stills singing in French against a chorus vaguely recalling 'Turn Back The Pages', only not as good. Dacus sings alternate lead, an ominous sign of things to come.

DIFFERENT TONGUES
A promising but ultimately average track, originally written by Stills and Dacus in London in October 1974, one month after CSN&Y's memorable show at Wembley Stadium. George Terry later suggested the key change, while Stills came up with the

string synthesizer arrangement.

SOLDIER

Stills plays piano, lead guitar and synthesizer on this song, which shared its title with a Neil Young composition. In Stills' version, the theme is the psychological plight of Vietnam Veterans, readjusting to civilian life.

THE LONER

Having covered 'New Mama' on his last album, Stills returned to the Neil Young song catalogue choosing a key track from the Canadian's debut solo album. Unfortunately, it's a passionless reworking.

STATELINE BLUES

A welcome acoustic number, which serves as a pleasant diversion. "Always seemed to end up with an acoustic tune on the album," Stills reflected. "Played it live on dobro for a few months, but it sounded richer on Maybelle, the oldest D-45, with just a dobro solo."

CLOSER TO YOU

Co-written by Stills, Dacus and Warner Schwebke, this featured Donnie on alternate lead vocal, a questionable decision in itself, although the mediocre quality of the material did nobody any great favours.

NO ME NIEGAS

"Lala had to play right on this one," Stills pointed out. "We tried to get a classic Latin feel and of course the holes in the percussion are as solid as the beats." Stills sings in Spanish, but the overall result is not as exciting as expected.

RING OF LOVE

Stills' decision to allow Dacus a vocal showcase of his own seemed a misguided act of generosity on an album already fatally weakened by poor material. "Flo and Eddie worked on him the better part of an evening until he forgot he wasn't supposed to be having a good time singing," Stills concluded.

CIRCLIN'

This Stills/Passarelli tune was recorded at LA's Cherokee Studios after they had completed basics and vocals for the album. Essentially, it's a thematic but brainless reworking of Joni Mitchell's 'The Circle Game'. An average rocker, inoffensive foot tapper and fairly banal ending to a disappointing album.

CROSBY NASH

WHISTLING DOWN THE WIRE

CROSBY & NASH

WHISTLING DOWN THE WIRE

ORIGINAL RELEASE DATE: JULY 1976

Released less than a year after the excellent *Wind On The Water*, this suffered by direct comparison. Structurally reminiscent of its predecessor, it was let down by generally weaker songs. Had the album been released at a different time, it might have seemed a little more rewarding in places but overall it was a case of more of the same, only not as good. Commercially, the work also dipped from the Top 20 heights of *Wind On The Water*, peaking at number 26 in the US album charts.

SPOTLIGHT

An ominous start to the album, inasmuch as this is less impressive than even the weakest track on *Wind On The Water*. Written by Danny Kootch and Nash, the lyrics reflect on the audience/performer relationship, but the melody sounds a little pedestrian.

BROKEN BIRD

Written by Crosby & Nash, with Graham on lead vocal, this proves one of the better tracks, with elliptical lyrics, and a line which provides the album's title.

TIME AFTER TIME

This slight Crosby ballad is sung in a whisper at times, with the emphasis on attempting to create an ambient mood. Lyrically compact, the impression is very much of a song still in fragmentary form.

DANCER

Part chant, part growl, this wordless piece from Crosby was certainly no 'Critical Mass'. The Section jam along towards the end and although interesting in parts, the piece lacks the enduring power of earlier experiments without words. At the time of its belated release, Nash was defiant about the work. "'Dancer' is a piece of music that Crosby's had for six or seven years and that we've tried cutting several times," he pointed out. "But it never happened. We tried, but CSN&Y weren't good enough musicians to cut 'Dancer'. I'm serious. They couldn't bother to take the time to learn the chords to it, and this is the first band I've ever worked with that could. That's really where it's at."

MUTINY

Not a song about dissension in the ranks of CSN&Y, as might be supposed from the title, but an evocative description of the Mutiny Hotel in Sailboat Bay, Miami. Nash's vocal is strong throughout, with the Section providing a long instrumental fade-out.

JB'S BLUES

Inspired by Nash's friendship with CSN&Y photographer Joel Bernstein, who "looked through glass at shooting stars", this was of mild autobiographical

interest. There was even a passing reference to the album "So Far", conveniently placed in inverted commas in case we missed the point. Alas, the song itself was rather lacklustre.

MAGUERITA

David Lindley's fiddle set the mood for another of Nash's passing paeans to a mysterious woman, recalling the theme of later songs like 'Carried Away'.

TAKEN AT ALL

Once intended for the Stills/Young project, this fascinating song documented the internecine strife within the CSN&Y ranks and the myriad of lost opportunities resulting from their inability to commit themselves to a single vision. In many ways this Crosby composition was a sister song to Nash's later 'Wasted On The Way'. For those in on CSN&Y puns, there is a sly reference to the failure of the "Human Highway" project. All things considered, this was arguably the best song on the album.

FOOLISH MAN

Structurally similar to 'Homeward Through The Haze' but substantially weaker as a song, this was one of Crosby's self-effacing reflections. Such humility would reach its apotheosis on the following year's 'Anything At All'.

OUT OF THE DARKNESS

Written by Crosby, Nash and Doerge, this at least provided a striking conclusion to the album. The string arrangement by Lee Holdridge added a dramatic touch, providing a suitably impressive finale. On reflection, it's a little ironic to hear Crosby singing a song of spiritual redemption in 1976 in the knowledge that he was soon to enter the darkness of heroin addiction and end the decade in a parlous state.

the
STILLS-YOUNG BAND

"LONG MAY YOU RUN"

STILLS-YOUNG BAND

LONG MAY YOU RUN

ORIGINAL RELEASE DATE: SEPTEMBER 1976

The idea of Stills & Young combining forces as a duo was initially an attempt to revive the spirit of Buffalo Springfield. Mid-way through the sessions for this album, however, Crosby & Nash were invited to participate and the first CSN&Y studio album since *Déjà Vu* seemed only months away. Instead, the sessions ended in bitterness and acrimony when Stills & Young abruptly decided to revert to the original concept and erased Crosby & Nash's contributions from the final recording. Public expectations were still high for a Stills/Young teaming, but the results proved terribly anti-climactic. Rather than the expected intense guitar interplay, Stills & Young offered a strangely subdued album of lacklustre songs, mostly inspired by their period in Hawaii. By the time the album was released the collaboration was long dead. A summer tour brought mixed reviews, then ended in farcical fashion when Young drove away after a gig leaving his partner a sarcastic note which read: "Dear Stephen, Funny how some things that start spontaneously end that way. Eat a peach, Neil".

LONG MAY YOU RUN

Young's famous tribute to his hearse opens the album on a buoyant note. The reference to Blind River conjures up memories of Young's period in The Squires while the topical reference to The Beach Boys frequently drew a burst of applause from audiences at his acoustic shows. Like many of the songs on this album, it's lightweight but charming.

MAKE LOVE TO YOU

Stills' rumination on romance, backed by Jerry Aiello on organ, has a late-night feel and, like much of the material on this album, is unusually restrained in its execution. Stills' lyrics are reasonably good, but there is a lack of passion in the work that makes a potentially excellent song sound merely good.

MIDNIGHT ON THE BAY

With its sparse backing and reflective but unarresting lyrics, this was obviously an exercise in understatement. Its appeal lies in an attractive melody but it's difficult to believe that Young spent much time on the composition.

BLACK CORAL

Again a good song, but peculiarly enervating, as if the album was systematically draining the participants of all passion. With energy levels at an inexplicable low, Stills relates a seduction of the deep in which he discovers Jesus at the bottom of the ocean, leading to the conclusion that "Heaven just might be the sea".

OCEAN GIRL

Stills makes his presence felt here with some wah-wah guitar but it's not enough to rescue a fairly inconsequential composition of two short verses. The song sounds undeveloped, as though Young was content to take some fragmentary allusions about drinking cocktails in the sun and attempt to conjure a suitably romantic setting.

LET IT SHINE

Young turns to gospel for a country song that sounds close to a parody. Not for the first time, he passes comment on contemporary religion, but here he can barely muster the usual indignation beyond a sarcastic, "Let them chant, let them chant".

12/8 BLUES

This was Stills' blues by numbers with a vague nod to 'Jet Set (Sigh)'. A filler by any other name, it did little to improve the quality of this album, which was in desperate need of something more arresting.

FONTAINEBLEAU

Strangely enough, the most urgent song on the album emerged from Young's almost paranoid loathing of a holiday resort. A reviewer once pondered with some justification why Young should get so upset about a hotel. Perhaps the

answer lies in the second verse in which Young explains: "I guess the reason I'm so scared of it is/I stayed there once and I almost fit/I left before I got out of it/People were drowning in their own Fontainebleau". Young's scathing observations inspire some of his familiarly anguished guitar playing, which is certainly rare on this album.

GUARDIAN ANGEL

This was an older song from Stills' catalogue, pleasant but wilfully unarresting as if the participants were intent on drowning even the possibility of any excitement on the album. It's a sobering thought to consider that this was the song which effectively broke up CSN&Y when they were on the brink of another important reunion. As Nash remembered from an earlier session: "Stephen had drunk a bottle of bourbon too many in my basement studio and he wanted me to sing a minor progression through a major chord change. Now I know I'm good and I knew that couldn't be done. So then Stephen made some nasty comments and I said, 'Hey, get the fuck out of my house'."

CROSBY, STILLS & NASH

CROSBY, STILLS & NASH

CSN

ORIGINAL RELEASE DATE: JUNE 1977

Eight years after the release of *Crosby, Stills & Nash*, the trio finally reconvened in their original incarnation for a much welcomed sequel. Released in the midst of the punk rock explosion in the UK, the work received middling reviews, while US critics, alienated by Stills' recent dip in form, seemed equally sceptical. However, for those capable of transcending the prejudices of the period, this was clearly the best album from the three participants in several years, eclipsing most of their recent releases as soloists and as a duo. That distinctive harmonic blend, a unique sound largely unparalleled in pop history, was back in abundance. Most impressive of all, Stephen Stills, whose form had declined so alarmingly of late, seemed determined to re-establish his reputation as a striking acoustic player and intelligent singer-songwriter. It was clear that the trio were following an old dictum by pooling their best current tunes for CS&N rather than selfishly holding back material for future solo projects. Sessions for the album went surprisingly smoothly and the maverick Neil Young was not missed. As Crosby noted at the time: "If he showed up right now he'd just weird it out. He can't do the painstaking vocals that we're doing right now." Public reaction to the record was extremely favourable and it soon climbed to an impressive number 2 in the US charts. The trio responded with an extensive US tour, their first ever under the CS&N banner. They had reached a fresh zenith at this point but, as ever, their future was anything but predictable.

SHADOW CAPTAIN

For the first and only time to date, Crosby is allowed the opening track on a CS&N album. This was another of his great songs from the Seventies, with those CS&N harmonies reaching heights previously heard on the best parts of their debut album and *Déjà Vu*.

The lingering final notes are among the most spine-tingling harmonies they've ever laid down. Craig Doerge's acoustic/electric piano accompaniment is also striking, while the lyrics are both mysterious and alluring. As Crosby remembers: "I was about 200 miles offshore… on my boat, and it was three in the morning. I woke up and wrote that entire set of lyrics word for word, and then went back to sleep. You've got to understand I had never thought of any image in that song or anything about that entire concept ever before."

SEE THE CHANGES

Back to his acoustic best, Stills resurrects the spirit of the first CS&N album, with this thoughtful ballad. The three-part harmonies were perfectly executed, while the material was a cut above Stills' recent solo work with some expressive playing and engagingly pensive lyrics.

CARRIED AWAY

This typically delicate Nash ballad echoed Stills' meditation with the words "moving through my changes". An attempt to capture the beauty of ephemeral attraction in an everyday situation, the song was inspired by Nash's brief fantasy fixation on a woman visiting a coffee shop in Miami. "My wife doesn't like that song," Nash confessed to *Song Talk*. "I saw this woman. We were never lovers, I never kissed her, I never touched her, but I loved her. I wanted to be carried away. I wanted to unshackle myself from everything that was in my life. And it was only a brief glimpse of a moment. But in that moment I wanted to be carried away and I wanted to go with this woman."

FAIR GAME

Another virtuoso acoustic display from Stills with strong Latin inflexions, this track underlined how much his audience had missed his playing and songwriting during the desultory *Illegal Stills* period.

ANYTHING AT ALL

Crosby's self-effacing humour was evident on this memorable composition in which he celebrates his self-opinionated personality. Light and airy, without a strong hook-line, it nevertheless fitted well on an album where reflective self-questioning was the dominant mood.

CATHEDRAL

A stark piano opening dramatizes the onset of an acid trip at Winchester Cathedral that Nash took while celebrating his 32nd birthday. The gripping narrative quickens pace in the fifth stanza during which he launches into an anti-religious diatribe, culminating in an identity crisis as he sees a gravestone of a person who died in 1799 on the same day and month that he was born. The LSD vision ended when Nash awoke to find himself at Stonehenge, slouched among the ruins. Piecing those experiences together to make a song proved a challenge. "It took four years to write 'Cathedral'," he told Paul Zollo. "It wouldn't finish itself. It was such an important topic for me, this realization that most of the world's wars to that point had been, in most part, created from religious differences: Spanish Inquisition, the Crusades, on and on... You couldn't utter the name of Jesus Christ and not realize what was done in

his name. That it wasn't all miracles and angels. That it was a great deal of death and darkness from people who took Jesus' name and used it in the wrong way. That's what 'Cathedral' is about."

DARK STAR

With Craig Doerge on jazzy piano, Joe Vitale on organ, and Stills resplendent on acoustic guitar, this sensual song was a passionate and eloquent apotheosis recalling earlier romantic infatuations with Judy Collins and Rita Coolidge. This time the woman's identity remained hidden, although Stills hinted that the sentiments were autobiographical.

JUST A SONG BEFORE I GO

While preparing to visit Hawaii, a friend challenged Nash to write a song on his piano in the short time they had left before driving to the airport. The result of that impromptu exercise was this US Top 10 hit. The line "travelling twice the speed of sound it's easy to get burned" was inspired by a trip on Concorde with a concomitant innuendo to cocaine abuse.

RUN FROM TEARS

Strong CS&N harmonies, plus some ear-catching rhythmic changes, elevate this otherwise straightforward Stills song into something more substantial. As the album reaches its denouement stage, he reverts to electric guitar for added emphasis.

COLD RAIN

This was written after Nash found himself back in Manchester freezing outside the Midland Hotel during a snowy afternoon. His mind commuted back to the late Fifties, when he and later Hollies' lead singer Allan Clarke had stood in the same spot eager to see the Everly Brothers in the flesh. The sense of déjà vu and realization that, despite all the changes to the city, people were still milling around as they had always done, sparked Nash's imagination. As he concluded: "I was so thankful that I'd had the instinct to want to get out of there and experience something my father had never experienced."

IN MY DREAMS

Crosby's allusive, unfocussed lyrics suggest that this could easily have been a wordless piece in the style of 'Song With No Words (Tree With No Leaves)'. Mid-way through the song, he appears to make a pertinent observation on the politics of CS&N: "Who gets breakfast? Who gets the lunch? Who gets to be the boss of this bunch? Who will steer?" The image of CS&N as a boat, well-manned or easily capsized, was carried over from the equally allusive 'Shadow Captain'.

I GIVE YOU GIVE BLIND

With Stills playing both acoustic piano and electric guitar and Mike Lewis adding a string arrangement, this was obviously intended as the album's grand finale. Although it is not Stills' greatest composition by a long way, the sheer exuberance and strength of performance carries the song along to a suitably dramatic conclusion.

CROSBY & NASH

CROSBY-NASH LIVE

ORIGINAL RELEASE DATE: NOVEMBER 1977

Timing is all-important with live albums and this was a work clearly out of time. Released by ABC to cash in on the recent CS&N get-together, it looked opportunist and unnecessary, with Crosby & Nash by then a distant memory. Viewed more sympathetically, it was an impressive souvenir of C&N's work with the so-called "Mighty Jitters", that formidable ensemble featuring David Lindley, Danny Kortchmar, Craig Doerge, Tim Drummond and Russ Kunkel. The musicianship throughout was strong and provided new depths to starker songs like 'Simple Man'. The much discussed highlight of the set was an experimental version of 'Déjà Vu', which stands as a lasting tribute to the continued invention of Crosby & Nash at a time when they were seemingly ostracized from Stills & Young and in need of a higher media profile. If a more complete version of this show could be unearthed, it would make a worthwhile and extremely impressive CD.

Full track listing: Immigration Man; Lee Shore; I Used To Be A King; Page 43; Fieldworker; Simple Man; Foolish Man; Mama Lion; Déjà Vu.

STEPHEN STILLS · THOROUGHFARE GAP

STEPHEN STILLS

THOROUGHFARE GAP

ORIGINAL RELEASE DATE: OCTOBER 1978

A strong candidate as the nadir of Stills' career, this was issued at a time when the individual members of CS&N were at their most unfashionable. Desperate to try something new in order to move on from their stereotypical image as mellow singer-songwriters, Stills took the bull by the horns and turned towards a disco beat, employing Mike Lewis, who had worked with the Bee Gees and Firefall. Stills' chances of reaping some unlikely commercial success were blighted by the poor quality of the material and the entire exercise was ridiculed by critics and scorned by most long-term fans. Stills' Latin forays had always been intriguing but here, amid a synthesized and antiseptic backing, all emotion in his music was systematically drained away.

YOU CAN'T DANCE ALONE

With Mike Lewis providing the strings and horns, Stills makes an uneasy attempt to switch from Latin to disco, complemented by Andy Gibb, Dave Mason and John Sambatero.

THOROUGHFARE GAP

This six-year-old song was originally a Manassas outtake, revamped with Al Gould on fiddle. Stills once referred to it as possibly his favourite work "from a literary viewpoint". However, the lyrics sound forced in places, despite Stills' recommendation.

WE WILL GO ON

Another ill-advised attempt at disco, with Mike Lewis drowning a rather average song with synthesized horns.

BEAUCOUP YUMBO

Stills attempts some cajun blues on one of the more catchy songs on the album. On virtually any other Stills release this would sound like mediocre filler; here it's among the better tracks on the album.

WHAT'S THE GAME

Gibb, Mason and Sambatero return for more falsetto swoops on another undemanding song. The lyric "hide behind walls" is borrowed from Stills' 'So Many Times'.

MIDNIGHT RIDER

A passable version of Gregg Allman's composition and easily superior to most of Stills' compositions on the album, although that is no great compliment.

WOMAN LLEVA

More horns, with vocalist Kitty Pritikin in the ascendant. Stills sings in Spanish, plays a Moog and attempts to find a groove on a song that never quite catches fire in spite of some distracting moments.

LOWDOWN

This was one of Stills' most depressing lyrics, uplifted by a seven-strong chorus, featuring Joe Vitale, George Perry, Mike

Finnigan, Brooks Honeycutt, Verna Richardson, Lisa Roberts. Stills joins them, adding a decent guitar solo to the proceedings.

NOT FADE AWAY

Another sign of waning inspiration, as Stills covers this Buddy Holly classic, made famous by the Rolling Stones in the Sixties. The best you can say about Stills' listenable interpretation is that he provides some new lyrics without seeking a publishing credit.

CAN'T GET NO BOOTY

Stills and Danny Kortchmar combine for this fun conclusion to the album in which they appear to parody soul and disco in the same breath. Stills' cod reference to "shaking my tail feather in your face" and the mindless refrain "can't get no booty" are part of the joke. Amusing, but inconsequential.

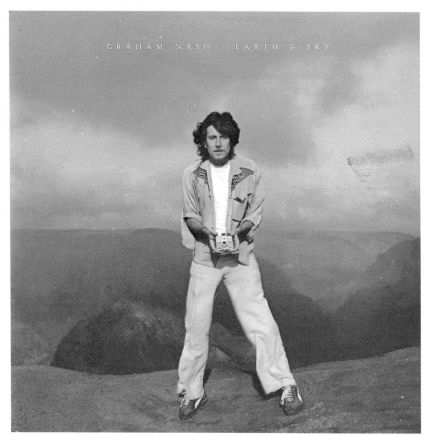

GRAHAM NASH · EARTH & SKY

GRAHAM NASH

EARTH AND SKY

ORIGINAL RELEASE DATE: 15 FEBRUARY 1979

By the late Seventies, CS&N were decidedly out of fashion as soloists. Nash was still in the fortunate position of being able to secure a record contract, but this release was largely ignored, and suffered both critically and commercially. Overall, it was an enervating work, reflective in tone, but lacking Nash's strongest material. Significantly, few of the songs featured would be retained for very long in his repertoire. Even if Nash had produced a stronger album, the times were against him at this point with New Wave acts ensuring a hard life for most of the decade's previously prominent singer-songwriters.

EARTH AND SKY

An unusually abstruse lyric from Nash, whose previous material had almost been transparently straightforward. Although not melodically that strong, the song was boosted by the presence of Joe Walsh on lead guitar and Cece Bullard on backing vocals.

LOVE HAS COME

Another slight ballad, this time with Steve Lukather on lead guitar. The delicate background vocals of Crosby, Jackson Browne, Nicolette Larson and Armando Hurley were introduced tentatively, while the song itself was evanescent in its scope and appeal.

OUT ON THE ISLAND

David Lindley's Hawaiian guitar set the mood for this track, which fitted in with the purposefully quiet ambience of the record. Even the backing vocalists Cleo Kennedy, Brenda Eager and Gloria Coleman sound noticeably restrained.

SKYCHILD

Nash's undemonstrative approach continued on this song, with Lindley carefully playing lead guitar while the backing singers hummed quietly in the background.

HELICOPTER SONG

Nash closed the first half of the album with this more upbeat work, buoyed by a formidable line-up of musicians, including Joe Vitale (percussion and timpani), Joe Lala (percussion), Joe Walsh (lead guitar), Stills and Danny Kortchmar (rhythm guitars), Craig Doerge (acoustic piano), Crosby and Leah Kunkel (backing vocals) and a five-piece string section.

BARREL OF PAIN
(HALF-LIFE)

Probably the best track on the album, this was a bitter commentary on the policy of disposing nuclear waste in the ocean. "I saw photographs of mutated sea life that had been exposed to the waste and I couldn't get the image out of my mind," Nash recalled. At one point in the song, he even imagines himself as a passive victim of nuclear fall-out before closing his poignant diatribe with an attack on money-making corporations.

T.V. GUIDE

Co-written by Nash and Joe Vitale, this slice of Orwellian doom was given some added bite by Craig Doerge's electric piano work and the employment of a 13-piece string section.

IT'S ALL RIGHT

A leftover from the 1974 CSN&Y tour, this was a slight composition, which worked reasonably well in concert, but was less distinguished as an album track.

MAGICAL CHILD

This was Nash at his most sickly sentimental, proclaiming the joys of fatherhood. Jackson Browne joins in on harmonica, aided by a full string section on a number that was surely too saccharine for all but the most committed to Nash's idyllic view of life.

IN THE 80'S

Nash closes the work on a suitably energetic note with an anthem dedicated to coming alive in the Eighties. The soaring backing vocals are exuberant, the melody catchy, but the lyrics betray a disconcerting vacuity, with Nash issuing a rallying call offering no substance to his complaints beyond some general sense of a national malaise.

CROSBY, STILLS & NASH

DAYLIGHT AGAIN

ORIGINAL RELEASE DATE: JUNE 1982

Although this album was an impressive and welcome return with strong songs and a US Top 10 placing, all was not as it seemed. Far from a democratic three-way effort, it was effectively a Stills/Nash album, with Crosby belatedly appearing as an add-on. The work effectively began after a Stills solo album, recorded with Barry Beckett, was rejected by CBS. Not long after, Stills played a one-off gig with Nash in Hawaii, and they so enjoyed the experience that plans were hatched for a joint album. It was a unique permutation that had yet to be tested. The duo paid for the sessions, gambling on a strong record company budget to follow. Unfortunately, Atlantic were more keen on a new CS&N product and encouraged the duo to bring back their erring partner. It proved an uneasy compromise. Although Crosby had an album full of rejected songs from his recent Capitol album, Stills & Nash only accepted one of his compositions, 'Delta' and a cover of 'Might As Well Have A Good Time'. Other compositions such as the stunning 'Distances', 'Drive My Car' and 'Melody' were not re-recorded, thereby creating a serious imbalance in the distribution of tracks. At one point, the 11-song album was set to include seven Stills compositions until a publishing dispute meant that one had to be dropped. Even then, he ended up with six tunes to Nash's three, with Crosby tagged on like an afterthought. Vocally, Crosby was slotted in where possible, but the album was still very much a two-way project with other harmony singers like Tim Schmit and Mike Finnigan filling his spaces. Given these various compromises, it was a relief that the album turned out so well, although the demotion of Crosby was a hard pill to swallow.

TURN YOUR BACK ON LOVE

Nash was practising some chords when Stills picked up on this song, which was completed with the assistance of Michael Stergis. All three play lead guitar on the track and Stills' vocal is extremely confident. Former Poco/Eagles vocalist Timothy B. Schmit effectively deputizes for Crosby in the harmony. A solid, catchy opening track.

WASTED ON THE WAY

Nash's penchant for writing hits was demonstrated with this bittersweet reflection on the up and down career of CSN&Y. Following 'Just A Song Before I Go' into the US Top 10, it confirmed Nash's crucial role in ensuring that the CS&N idyll remained part of the public consciousness, despite changing fashions in the music industry. Wayne Goodwin's fiddle break was a surprise and effective addition.

SOUTHERN CROSS

Stills' power as a lyricist appeared to have diminished since the mid-Seventies, but here he was presented with a potentially great song

by Richard and Michael Curtis. Originally titled 'Seven League Boots', the track needed some additional work. "It drifted around too much," Stills explained. "I re-wrote a new set of words and added a different chorus, a story about a long boat trip I took after my divorce. It's about using the power of the universe to heal your wounds. Once again, I was given somebody's gem and cut and polished it." He also provided a powerful and expressive vocal, reinforced by some strong harmony work courtesy of Mike Finnigan and Tim Schmit.

INTO THE DARKNESS

This Nash composition was a late addition to the album's running order, after Stills' 'Feel Your Love' was removed for fear of a plagiarism suit by Rose Royce. Although Nash was coy about the theme of the song, it seemed a transparent warning to Crosby about the tragedy of his fall into drug addiction. Using nautical imagery to ram the message home, Nash offered the poignant verse: "I see your face it is ghostly pale/Into the sunset we are watching you sail". The song neatly articulated the frustrations and fears of Crosby's friends, ending with the warning "Stay out of the darkness". Crosby was indignant about the decision to include the track on the album, having already resisted various attempts to mend his ways.

DELTA

Proof that Crosby's muse was still active, even in the twilight of his drug addiction, was evidenced by this remarkable song. Unusually for Crosby, this was written on piano and might have remained in artistic limbo if Jackson Browne hadn't coaxed him to complete the work during an evening at Warren Zevon's home. Even by Crosby's standards, it was an exceptional work and probably the last indisputably great song he wrote before drugs consumed his creative urges.

SINCE I MET YOU

Composed by Stills and Stergis, this was the only song recorded from scratch following Crosby's late recruitment to the sessions. Effervescent and upbeat, it displayed Stills' more commercial side, although the lyrics were less than arresting.

TOO MUCH LOVE TO HIDE

Stills was stretching himself very thin by including this collaboration with Gerry Tolman. It was reasonable enough but largely inconsequential and merely filled a gap where another Crosby song could easily have been slotted.

SONG FOR SUSAN

Nash's heartfelt tribute to his wife Susan was a sentimental ballad made interesting by an exotic arrangement and a lengthy supporting cast, including Jay Ferguson on organ and a four-piece cello section.

YOU ARE ALIVE

Taken from Stills' doomed CBS album, this song was almost identical in theme to Nash's 'Song For Susan', relating the healing power of relationships, a fear of loneliness and the need to face the dangers of a lack of emotional fulfilment. Nash adds a suitably wistful harmonica break.

MIGHT AS WELL HAVE A GOOD TIME

Ironically, the only other song that Crosby was

allowed to include from his rejected solo album was not even one of his own compositions, but an upbeat reflection on life from Judy Henske and Craig Doerge. While 'Distances' or 'Drive My Car' would have been preferable, this *carpe diem* ballad nevertheless enhanced the positive mood of the album and was a rare example of unadulterated CSN harmonies.

DAYLIGHT AGAIN

Here, at last, was one of the great lost Stills' songs from the early Seventies. As he explained: " 'Daylight Again' was actually a precursor to 'Find The Cost Of Freedom', but for years all I had was the tune and the first line, 'Daylight again, following me to bed...' I was out on tour and we'd done four nights running. I was in Williamsburg, Virginia, drunk and burnt out and dead tired. At the end of the concert I began to play the song. I didn't have any words, but I continued to play. I closed my eyes and went into a trance and saw a movie. It was a talking dream where I went back 112 years, to the Civil War. The lyrics just flowed from me like an automatic poem. I sang them as they came into my head and the whole story unfolded." It was a major revelation to hear a

song that had existed almost as folk memory for the past 10 years. Stills' enchanting acoustic guitar playing and the inventive banjo solo prior to the final section of the song merely added to the highlights. Crosby was so impressed with Art Garfunkel's harmony on the track that he felt it would be sacrilege to insist on deleting his work and substituting his own. As a closing album track this was exceptional. Perhaps the only negative point to make is the observation that the original live recordings were even more dramatic. In concert, Stills would evoke the spirit of the Civil War, with lines like: "They didn't know what else to do, except fight the men in blue/So they came and so the blood was spilt in the morning dew". In other verses he would tell of musket, sword and cannon and simple farmers, before speculating on modern warfare and mass communication. Invariably, the Manassas version would end with Stills screaming out 'Find The Cost Of Freedom', stretching syllables like a blues shouter, after which the entire ensemble would reconvene for a solemn final refrain. On the album version, all this is regrettably curtailed, but the track is still one of the best and most welcome songs in the unit's catalogue.

CROSBY, STILLS & NASH

ALLIES

ORIGINAL RELEASE DATE: JUNE 1983

Despite Crosby's creative incapacitation, CS&N continued their round of touring and new product was required. This hotchpotch of a release was essentially a live album, preceded by two new studio tracks, Stills' 'War Games' and the Stills/Nash collaboration 'Raise A Voice', whose lyrics included an allusion to Stephen's 'We Are Not Helpless'. Significantly, Crosby was not involved in these recordings. The live songs were taken from their appearance at the Universal Amphitheatre, Universal City, over Thanksgiving weekend, 1982. Those concerts would also provide footage for the video *Daylight Again*. All things considered, the material on *Allies* was fairly good and after hearing the versions of 'For Free' and 'Shadow Captain' many listeners will have consoled themselves that Crosby's voice wasn't shot as rumours suggested. Unfortunately, a closer look at the small print on the record revealed that the two Crosby songs were not from the Universal show but had been borrowed from a performance in Houston, Texas, in 1977. That said everything about Crosby's state in the early Eighties when his functioning in CS&N was little more than a cynical illusion.

Full track listing: War Games; Raise A Voice; Turn Your Back On Love; Barrel Of Pain (Half-Life); Shadow Captain; Dark Star; Blackbird; For Free; Wasted On The Way; For What It's Worth.

STEPHEN STILLS

RIGHT BY YOU

ORIGINAL RELEASE DATE: AUGUST 1984

Having let his solo career slip during the second half of the Seventies, Stills, like Crosby and Nash, found it difficult to secure a major deal during the Eighties. While CS&N as a unit were guaranteed a certain level of sales, solo work was a considerable risk for record company investment. This was Stills' big chance to make an impression and, for such an important release at such a crucial time in his career, it was a bitter disappointment, fatally compromised by an insipid, synthetic AOR production. You need only play this back to back with *Stephen Stills* to acknowledge its paucity of imagination and woeful lack of songwriting prowess. One of the great mysteries of Stephen Stills' career was how he was able to produce works of such consistent excellence for the whole of the first half of the Seventies and then founder so badly thereafter. For those of us who argued that he was one of the most important, original and stylistically inventive singer-songwriters of his era, not to mention a guitarist of exceptional skill, this release added nothing to his reputation.

50/50

This effervescent Latin-influenced track, composed by Stills and Joe Lala, featured three percussionists, some heavy brass and prominent piano. Funnily enough, it was guest guitarist Jimmy Page whose clinical playing most detracted from the feel of the song, which was an otherwise fair opener.

STRANGER

Co-written by Stills and his son Christopher, this was spoilt by the synthetic, period production of the Albert Brothers, whose attempts to invest the song with a "modern sound" drained it of real worth.

FLAMING HEART

Written by Ray Arnott, this featured both Bernie Leadon and Jimmy Page. An enjoyable enough guitar romp, but the song was a pretty basic boogie of no great merit.

LOVE AGAIN

More mid-Eighties high gloss production creating a sanitized feel to a song that never takes off despite boasting Stills' latest non-romantic philosophy: "Love is an accident of faith".

NO PROBLEM

The formulaic sound continues here with the production reducing Stills to the level of a mere functionary on his own record.

CAN'T LET GO

At last Stills' voice cuts through the aural mire on this Joe Esposito/Al Willis composition. Unfortunately, alternate verses are passed over to soulful Mike Finnigan, whose presence prevents us from hearing Stills alone. The execution is slick enough but it's difficult to avoid the stigma of AOR anonymity.

GREY TO GREEN

Co-written by Stills and James Newton Howard, this had a slight reggae tinge, with unintentionally amusing lyrics about a woman blessed with multi-coloured, kaleidoscopic eyes. A pleasant enough track.

ONLY LOVE CAN BREAK YOUR HEART

This was the third solo album on which Stills included a Neil Young cover. Not the most original choice, I fear, and Stills' reading is less than required listening, despite the presence of a new sixth verse.

NO HIDING PLACE

Chris Hillman and Herb Pedersen join Stills for a rare piece of country eclecticism on this 1963 composition about the Bomb. The lyrics are highly amusing and the playing good. If only there had been a little more stylistic adventurousness on this album, Stills might have produced something worthwhile.

RIGHT BY YOU

Assisted by Jimmy Page, Stills concludes matters with a blues excursion. The song is unremarkable, but at least there's some belated emotional authenticity here, which is long overdue.

GRAHAM NASH

INNOCENT EYES

GRAHAM NASH

INNOCENT EYES

ORIGINAL RELEASE DATE: APRIL 1986

Still burned by the memory of the commercial failure of *Earth And Sky*, Nash knew that he was unlikely to succeed with a straightforward singer-songwriter album, so elected to try something radically new. The results came as quite a shock. As Nash explained: "A lot of people have said to me that they thought the record company put the wrong record into the sleeve. I took it as a compliment because one of the things I wanted to do with this record was change the preconception of who I am... I wanted to change what I do also. That's why I used four songs written by other people which I haven't done in 20 odd years." While Nash's decision to try something that sounded fresh and contemporary was commendable, the experiment backfired. The work sounded derivative of current trends rather than genuinely innovative and, not surprisingly, alienated old listeners, while attracting few new ones. Without a hit single, Nash had little hope of reinventing himself and the work was largely ignored, leaving him in commercial limbo. He has not recorded a solo album since.

SEE YOU IN PRAGUE

In a concerted attempt to break free from his mellow singer-songwriter image, Nash opens the album with this synth-based, linn-drum dominated track from the pens of Davitt Siegerson and Richie Zito. "It's a kind of 1986 'Marrakesh Express' with a few spies thrown in," Nash noted.

KEEP AWAY FROM ME

Nash is again swamped by linn drums and keyboards on this acerbic comment on greed in the record industry. "This particular guy tried to get me to play Sun City in South Africa," Nash recalled. "CS&N were offered $800,000 to do three nights' work and he thought that was cool." Needless to say, CS&N declined the offer.

INNOCENT EYES

This was written by English songwriter Paul Bliss and originally intended for The Hollies' reunion album. It was then passed over to Air Supply, who also neglected to include it on their album. Realizing that the song was still available, Nash bought the original 24-track from Bliss, who appears as bassist on the track. Kenny Loggins was then recruited as guest vocalist. The overall effect is to recreate Nash in a new guise that still sounds strangely anonymous.

CHIPPIN' AWAY

Nash attempts some synthesized reggae on this Ted Fedora number. "I liked what it said," Nash noted. "We so often put walls around our feelings and our eyes and emotions that we should learn to slowly chip them away." One significant aspect of the recording was that it later provided a catchy tune and slogan for CS&N when they appeared at the Berlin Wall.

OVER THE WALL

Nash deliberately sequenced the album so that this track about the Berlin Wall followed 'Chippin' Away'. As expected Nash used the wall as a metaphor for the distance in human relationships. Speaking more directly, he observed: "It's a preposterous piece of architecture and an affront to human dignity and I'd like to tear it down myself, brick by brick."

DON'T LISTEN TO THE RUMORS

This John Palermo composition, featuring Kate Yester on additional vocal, sounded very much like US AOR material. Nash liked the song, even equating its title with the history of press rumours about CSN&Y.

SAD EYES

Written about Susan Nash, while she lay asleep, this was a typically pleasant ballad which sounded as though it had been channelled through a food mixer of special effects. James Taylor can be heard amid the production melee on additional vocals.

NEWDAY

An upbeat but irritating song, this Nash/Doerge number was originally discarded then reinstated for questionable inclusion on the album.

GLASS AND STEEL

The best song on the album was this reflection on the lifestyle of Crosby. Nash found inspiration in the suitably austere setting of a Milan hotel room in 1983. As he remembered: "It was an intense period of thought about David and his problems and how I could deal with it myself and help him deal with it. I began to realize that no matter what anybody thinks about what David's problem is and he's taken a lot of grief in the past, especially the past few years, it's worse for David. Nobody knows how bad it is really, except David. People should try and remember that."

I GOT A ROCK

Nash's simple, sloganeering lyrics end the album on a slight note, rescued by a treble keyboard assault from Graham, Craig Doerge and Alan Pasqua. "It was a difficult song to write," Nash insisted. "It's not easy to wax poetical about such a devastating subject as a nuclear arms race... It's not easy writing simple songs... it's harder to cut everything away than it is to just babble... It's a child's song, I wrote it for the children."

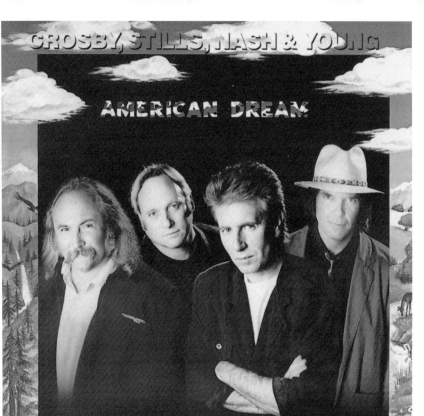

CROSBY, STILLS, NASH & YOUNG

AMERICAN DREAM

ORIGINAL RELEASE DATE: NOVEMBER 1988

It was widely publicized that, in the event of Crosby overcoming his heroin addiction, Young would record another CSN&Y album. Initially, there were problems with Geffen Records concerning contractual releases but once Young moved back to Reprise the reunion was unstoppable. What next emerged was a mirror image of events in 1974. Back then, the quartet had undertaken a massive stadium tour but, frustratingly, failed to complete a studio album. This time around there would be an album, but no attendant tour. Recording began as early as April 1987 with Nash's 'Shadowland', but the bulk of the album was completed in the spring and autumn of the following year

Ultimately, the work received a mixed reception and the lack of a tour ensured that it was not widely promoted, despite its early chart success. Almost inevitably, Young's contributions were assumed to be the most interesting, but this was not the case. Throughout he was matched and often bettered by his fellow members, just as he had been on much of *Déjà Vu*. What the album lacked from Young was a contribution to match the grandeur of 'Country Girl', the passion of 'Ohio', the ingenuity of 'Everybody I Love You' or the mystery of 'Pushed It Over The End'. CS&N urgently needed Young's passion and grit in order to produce the record of a lifetime. Instead, they received his softer side. It was as if he'd forgotten about the electric power he had brought to 'Almost Cut My Hair' and now regarded CS&N as the vehicle for his cosier, predominantly harmonic work. Overall, the album was still strong and at nearly an hour in length provided enough opportunity for the participants to show off their talents. It was actually far better than many of us anticipated and showcased the enduring viability of CSN&Y as a creative unit. Regrettably, another reunion has proven frustratingly elusive.

AMERICAN DREAM

The title track of the album seemed to be inspired by the fall of Jerry Lee Lewis' cousin, the celebrated evangelist Jimmy Swaggart. Young's narrative is a wry look at the private and public reaction to the scandal. In determining where "things went wrong", Young points the finger at the American Dream itself. Hypocrisy and hubris go hand in hand here and the protagonist seems both the subject of fun and sympathy. Musically, the track was most notable for its engaging melody, synthed pipes and glorious CS&N harmonies at key moments in the song. Indeed, when issued as a single, this brought them a minor hit in the UK.

GOT IT MADE

This surprisingly commercial track featured Stills on vocal and keyboards, with Young providing the electric guitar. It was vaguely reminiscent of their work in the Stills/Young Band, but more impressive. Lyrically, this was Stills' strongest composition on the album, although there were signs that his song lexicon had been well thumbed with phrases like

"set of changes" and "it doesn't matter" recalling past glories.

NAME OF LOVE

Here Young uncharacteristically offered a message to world rulers: "Do it in the name of love". In keeping with the CS&N ethos he warned against the dangers of missiles, a somewhat contradictory view considering his pro-nuclear statements earlier in the decade. Then again, Young was never renowned for his consistency of viewpoint. Musically, the song offered a chance to hear Stills and Young trading guitar solos, though not to any spectacular effect. In fact the real hero here was Joe Vitale whose exceptional drumming gave the song its edge.

DON'T SAY GOODBYE

This lachrymose Nash ballad was his sole attempt at a love song on the album. Crosby, of all people, was conspicuous by his absence from the credits, which featured Stills, Young and Joe Vitale. Like many Nash songs, this tended towards the mawkish, but elsewhere on the album he would show a surprising diversity in his choice of theme veering more towards social concerns than personal angst.

THIS OLD HOUSE

CS&N provided the high harmonies while Young controlled the music, assisted by synth programmer Bruce Bell. Lyrically, the song deals with the power of the banks in repossessing property. Young sentimentalizes the issues with a *House On The Prairie* lyric in which kids play on swings, mother tends the garden and the parents plan a kitchen on the spot where they first made love. As far as CSN&Y are concerned it's the musical context that's the problem. The superstar foursome sound ill suited to a straight country arrangement of this nature. This song would have been appropriate for *Old Ways* and better served by the International Harvesters. At least some critics made an amusing connection by linking the composition with Nash's 'Our House' for which it was, intentionally or otherwise, a witty response.

NIGHTTIME FOR THE GENERALS

This was an acerbic, hard-hitting diatribe in the spirit of 'Long Time Gone' and 'Almost Cut My Hair'. Many nominated this as the best track on the album and it was a great pleasure to witness Crosby at his most angry, sneering contemptuously at the corruption of a military elite. Stills provided additional edge to the track with a strong lead guitar solo, the inspiration for which he credited to "James Marshall Hendrix".

SHADOWLAND

Co-written by Nash, Vitale and Rick Ryan, this track revealed Nash's continued willingness to use modern recording technology, including various sound effects and synth drums. His reflections on the casualties of war were powerful and poignant, confirming his continued strength as a songwriter.

DRIVIN' THUNDER

Although credited to Stills & Young, it's difficult to imagine what the latter contributed, lyrically or musically. Stills takes the lead vocal, with Young detectable in the chorus. The song proved nothing special – more a vehicle for Stills to enjoy a spiky lead guitar break. More fun than fascinating, this whimsical car song was similar in theme to Crosby's 'Drive My Car', both songs testifying in some ways to an arrested adolescence in their fixation on the juvenile love of driving.

CLEAR BLUE SKIES

Nash's ecological concerns were already well-known and here he returns to one of his favourite themes. The attractive melody served as a pleasant contrast to the two Stills' uptempo numbers in which it was framed.

THAT GIRL

Stills attempts some slick AOR with Young's Bluenotes deputizing for the Memphis Horns of old. Unfortunately, the banal, lightweight lyrics fail to do justice to Stills. As Crosby frankly noted: "I'm not all that happy about the stuff we got out of Stills. I don't think we got the best that we could get out of Stephen. I would have liked to have seen stronger songs. Remember this is the guy who wrote 'Carry On', 'Suite: Judy Blue Eyes' and 'Helplessly Hoping'. There isn't an acoustic guitar song from him on the album."

COMPASS

This haunting song of redemption, written while Crosby was still languishing in a Texas jail, was proof positive of his creative resurgence although boasts of newly-discovered prolific writing skills were to prove exaggerated. Here he is at his best, playing acoustic guitar and singing in a voice that is both languid and full of restrained passion. Young's harmonica and Stills' beautifully executed harmony enhance the spooky ambience. Lyrically, Crosby was back in the ascendant, except for one appalling slip of the pen when his similes plummeted into unintended comic bathos: "I have seized death's door handle/Like a fish out of the water/Waiting for the mercy of the cat". The implied image of a fish seizing a door handle was something that Crosby clearly failed to notice. Those three lines aside, the song was one of his best with an arrangement that was masterful in its ingenuity.

SOLDIERS OF PEACE

With synths and choruses at the ready, Nash made his grandest gesture with this anti-war plea. It's akin to a rock 'Onward Christian Soldiers', employing the military metaphor as a plea for peace. Stills throws in a brief but uplifting solo and the song concludes in spectacular fashion with a 21-piece choir screaming "No more", thereby repeating the message of Nash's other great anti-war anthem, 'Military Madness'. In noting the origins of 'Soldiers Of Peace', Nash explained: "A friend of mine had been making a film about Vietnam veterans who were travelling to Nicaragua and talking with the soldiers there about the futility of war. They were pointing out to these soldiers how they had been lied to by their own government, and ignored when they returned home. One of these veterans was Scott Camil, about whom I'd written 'Oh, Camil! (The Winter Soldier)'. At the same time, David and I had been invited to play at a Vietnam Veterans' benefit and, like many Americans, we went to the Vietnam Memorial. It makes most people who walk down it cry before they get half-way, and the reason is very simple: there are too many names on that wall. This song came out of these experiences, and was written for all

the people who fight for peace."

FEEL YOUR LOVE

Another predominantly solo effort from Young, with musical assistance from Joe Vitale. Although slight, it was a pretty melody and typical of the type of material that Young associated with CS&N. Once again, the placing of the track on the album seemed designed to lighten the mood after the intensity of Nash's explosive anthem. Like Stills, Young had his favourite phrases and this would not be the last time he used the "mansion on the hill" line.

NIGHT SONG

The final track on the album was a work of brooding intensity written by Stills and Young. Stills' lead vocal is impressive and convincing, while Young provides a passionate and gritty edge to the chorus. What proves most memorable is the intense, interweaving lead guitar work from the two which outclasses anything on the Stills/Young album and reminds us of how important their partnership was at its peak. A salutary end to a memorable album.

OH YES I CAN
David Crosby

DAVID CROSBY

OH YES I CAN

ORIGINAL RELEASE DATE: FEBRUARY 1989

When Capitol Records rejected Crosby's second solo album in 1981 it seemed that all we would hear of that work would be 'Delta' and 'Might As Well Have A Good Time', which were included on *Daylight Again*. Fortunately, his rehabilitation and high media profile ensured that the lost work was at last completed. The quality of Crosby's contributions to *American Dream* prompted some commentators to suggest that this new work might turn out to be a work of brilliance in the vein of *If I Could Only Remember My Name*. That was a delusion partly resulting from Crosby's over-enthusiastic comments about his personal creative resurgence in the wake of drug addiction. The prosaic truth was that he still found it difficult to write an album full of songs to order, as this work demonstrated. No new barriers were broken here, but there were enough high moments to satisfy Crosbyphiles long starved of product. The main criticism of the album was its tendency towards prettiness and occasional production lapses into the realms of over slick, radio-friendly AOR. Crosby at his best was always a tortured soul and while it was pleasing to see him happily married with a renewed zest for life, some of his old power seemed lost on this new set of songs. In all probability, he needed a little more time to round off the album with a couple of top class songs, but with a major autobiography to promote it was necessary to complete the work to a hard deadline.

DRIVE MY CAR

Originally scheduled for Crosby's unreleased 1981 album, this track was re-recorded with a more contemporary production to kick-start the album. Leland Sklar's synth and Danny Kortchmar's guitar provided the gloss as Crosby offered a suitably energetic vocal performance. It's a relief to hear that Crosby the driver "was not out looking for honeys" but his fascination with cars inevitably conjured up the well-publicized crashes and arrests that he suffered in the Eighties. At the height of his freebasing addiction, Crosby learned how to drive with his feet in order not to miss a toke from his ever present pipe.

MELODY

In April 1980, Crosby rummaged through his bag and pulled forth a sheaf of lyrics, which included a new song, 'Melody'. He told me that he intended to record this song for his next album and proceeded to read out the lyrics with some pride. It was to be the last song that he completed for several years. Given the subject matter – a love song to music – it was ironic that the composition heralded his entry into a long period of drug-induced writer's block. Revived for this album, the song was a little too slick and sentimental for its own good. Co-writer Craig Doerge played synth, which merely added to the sterile feel of a track that would probably have fared better as a more sparse acoustic reading.

MONKEY AND THE UNDERDOG

"I got a live track and no overdubs," Crosby enthused about this track. One of the first of his reflections on his battle with drug addiction, the song was compromised by a leaden arrangement, complete with an overwrought rhythm section and overdone organ.

IN THE WIDE RUIN

Written by Craig Doerge and Judy Henske, this was a class song, beautifully performed by Crosby, who sings with great feeling. Jackson Browne assists on the harmonies on this welcome return to form.

TRACKS IN THE DUST

A strong ballad with some impressive acoustic guitar accompaniment, this song began as a conversation at a dinner party which Crosby transferred into verse. The result was another high point of the album.

DROP DOWN MAMA

A familiar song from his live shows and collaborations with The Grateful Dead in 1970, this bar room blues was never really suited to Crosby's voice or style. Its main purpose was to liven up crowds in small clubs and bars who could only handle so much singer-songwriter angst. Not an obvious or appropriate candidate for a much-vaunted solo album, so why did he revive this second-rate number? "It was fun," Crosby told me. "My compatriots in making the record said: 'Why don't you do 'Drop Down Mama? You bark the hell out of it, and it's a good tune.' It's just an old folk tune I do for laughs. They said, 'Well, you may do it for laughs but everybody else likes it for rock. It's a shuffle, it cooks along… put it on the record'. So they browbeat me into it. I think we got what we got because Jim Keltner played on it."

LADY OF THE HARBOR

In the early Eighties, Crosby was dubbed "Man of the Year" in *Rolling Stone* for his apparently anti-authoritarian exploits in the face of an impending jail sentence. It was a surprise therefore to hear him extolling America as the promised land for immigrants and home of freedom. "There's no question that 'Lady Of The Harbor' is a flag-waver," he admitted to me. "It's talking about the ideals and I am an idealist. It came out of me and I thought, 'This is pretty flag-waving stuff'. Then I said: 'No, it's valid. I believe this shit'. So I put it on the record. I'm not ashamed of it. The song came out pretty well, largely because of how prettily Bonnie Raitt sang on it."

DISTANCES

Although a decade old and unchanged from the original submitted to Capitol, this was still the best song on the album. The use of two pianos, courtesy of Kenny Kirkland and Graham Nash, added majesty to the piece. Crosby's phrasing was excellent and demonstrated that, even in the sad depths of drug addiction, he was still able to create a song of great beauty. The theme was also an old favourite – detailing the distances between human beings and the problems of communication, both personal and political.

FLYING MAN

This was also unchanged from the original Capitol album. Although less atmospheric than the superior choral work on *If I Could Only Remember My Name*, it remained a strong addition to this album. Explaining his decision to leave 'Distances' and 'Flying Man' unaltered after a gap of approximately nine years, Crosby admitted: "I liked them so much that I didn't want to mess with them. I couldn't see how I could change them. I was thrilled with what Larry Carlton played on it and I felt the vocals came out really well, so I left those tunes exactly as they were."

OH YES I CAN

The album's title track was another superior cut on an occasionally patchy record. "It's one of the few songs I wrote on piano and I really love it," Crosby told me. "It's mostly autobiographical, but in the first verse where it says, 'The woman I thought I was in love with' is absolutely not true. But the rest of it is very autobiographical and the title describes how I feel about the record." Not so much a denial of his past, but an affirmation of his power in the present, this was very much a love song to his wife Jan, who had stuck with him through the worst of times. The realization that they had both survived scarcely believable bouts of drug abuse encouraged fleeting impressions of omnipotence. "I had a lot of that feeling at the time," Crosby admitted. "A lot of: 'Hey, I didn't die. Well, I can do anything now.' It's an amazing experience, man. To be pretty well convinced that you're going to die any minute, because that's what happens to junkies. Junkies die. And then to have it not happen, you suddenly go, 'Oh, gee, I'm still here! This is kind of fun. What do I do now?'"

MY COUNTRY 'TIS OF THEE

The album closed with a traditional song arranged by Michael Hedges and featuring Graham Nash and J.D. Souther on backing vocals. Another pleasant flag-waver, it seemed strangely out of character for a radical like Crosby, who had previously spent much of his life denouncing the state of America in songs like 'Long Time Gone' and 'Almost Cut My Hair'. "Some people are very puzzled by that," he told me. "In our country, you have to make a very sharp delineation between the policies of the elected administration and the principles of the country, the ideals of the country, the Constitution, the Bill of Rights and the core thinking of the people that started the country. I feel very strong towards the principles of the country whereas I disagree vehemently with a lot of the policies. I have all the way down the line and have been very vocal about it."

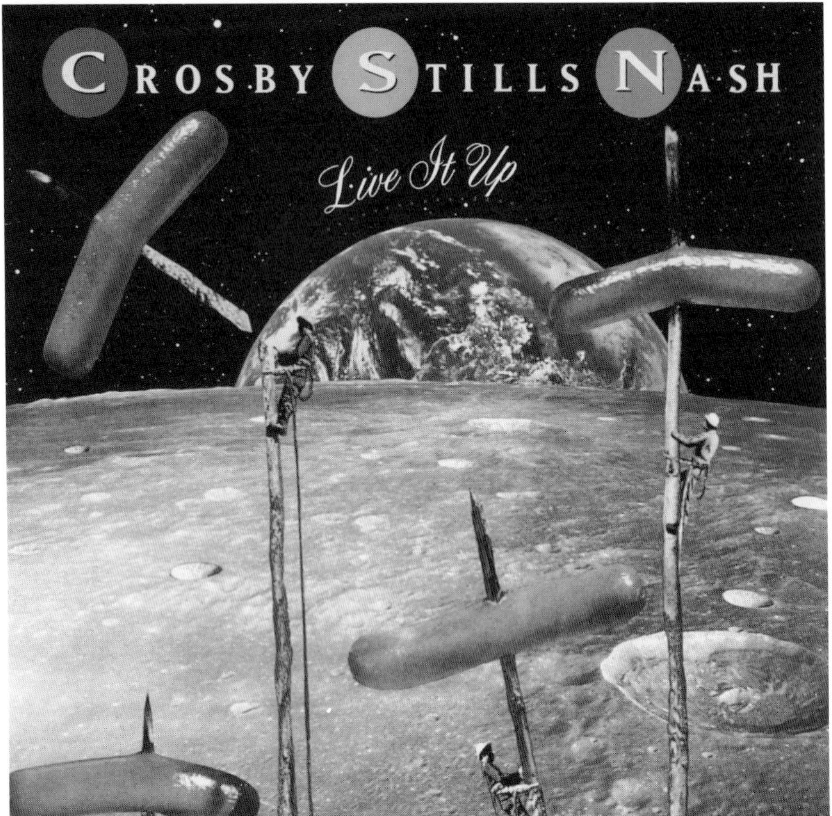
CROSBY STILLS NASH
Live It Up

CROSBY, STILLS & NASH

LIVE IT UP

ORIGINAL RELEASE DATE: JUNE 1990

If ever a record was damned by its sleeve, then this one deserved its fate. The artwork appalled many, some of whom took to wondering whether the impaled four sausages were meant to be some oblique comment on CSN&Y as much as a dig at American imperialism. As for the album itself, it was generally agreed that this was easily the least impressive CS&N release to date. Part of the problem was that it had not been intended as a three-way effort until late in the proceedings. "It started out as a Crosby & Nash record," Graham admitted. "David and I cut nine things and then we would wait for Stephen to see if he could add three or four things of his own and we could turn it into a CS&N record, and that's exactly what happened." The artificial way the album was conceived was reflected in its lack of consistency. Stills' efforts were not his strongest, while Crosby, not for the first time, appeared muted, with only a couple of songs to his name. Given his much-touted creative renaissance in the wake of a decade of drug abuse, this was not much of an advertisement for sobriety. Nash was the dominant force here, but there was a tendency to rely on outside writers and players, as if CS&N no longer believed in their own ability to reflect their times. The sound was upbeat and modern, but there was also a hollowness at the centre of the work and several good songs were lost and largely forgotten amid the distracting bombast of a high gloss production.

LIVE IT UP

The opening track on the album was written solely by Joe Vitale, with Nash on lead vocal. Bombastic but catchy, the production included synth bass and synth guitar and an overpowering choral backing by the Williams family.

IF ANYBODY HAD A HEART

Amazingly, this was also a song written outside the CS&N camp, this time by J.D. Souther and Danny Kortchmar. Nash again took lead vocal, with Crosby's former Byrds' partner Roger McGuinn on Rickenbacker guitar. Like many of the songs on this album, the effect was a little overblown in places and the absence of CS&N in the writing credits was more than disconcerting.

TOMBOY

This was a below average composition from Stills, with Joe Vitale's synth drums and bass again in evidence. In discussing why he wrote such a juvenile number, Stills offered some unsolicited views on women: "It always seemed to me that all the great girls got these neanderthals with no brains but terrific bodies... Tomboys are my favourite kind of girls and they always end up getting their hearts broken chasing these absolute dolts."

HAVEN'T WE LOST ENOUGH

Co-written by Stills and Kevin Cronin at a time when they were both recovering from broken relationships, this emerged as an impressive acoustic track. "While commiserating with each other one night we decided to write a song," Stills remembered. "We finished it in the studio one night several years later, and recorded it the next day. With acoustic music, there's no place to hide." For all its merits, the song sounded a little incongruous among all the synth rock.

YOURS AND MINE

When Crosby first wrote this song, the melody provided by Craig Doerge failed to match the words, so they tried again. Eventually, Nash was recruited to "upgrade the lyrics" and the song was completed. Crosby's primary inspiration remained intact throughout. As he remembered: "The original idea came from me looking at a picture of a kid who was maybe 12 years old and standing with an AK 47, and very proud of it. I said, 'How can we have gotten everything so wrong that this could happen?.... Obviously, we have made a mistake'."

(GOT TO KEEP) OPEN

This was the last song recorded for the album and, according to Nash, "a struggle to get it the way we wanted it". Bruce Hornsby was recruited on piano and organ, and the song emerged with a strong reggae tinge. Although listenable enough, it was ultimately fairly bland by Stills' higher standards.

STRAIGHT LINE

This was written by Tony Beard, who also played lead guitar alongside Stills. "Stephen found it difficult to play a cohesive solo through those changes," Nash noted. "It wasn't quite his thing." In order to vary the sound, Peter Frampton was commandeered to play the solo. Nash sang the lyrics exceptionally well, but you have to ask whether the material was really suitable for CS&N and would they not have been better recording one of their own songs.

HOUSE OF BROKEN DREAMS

The antithesis of 'Our House', this Nash composition was inspired by a chance remark by Dave Gilmour. During a torrid time in his personal life, Nash's wife phoned him one day, only to be greeted by the reply, "Hello… house of broken dreams". The words were enough to coax a sympathetic ballad from Nash.

ARROWS

"The beginning of this song came to me in a dream," Crosby explained. "I can almost never remember what happens to me in dreams but the first couple of lines of the song I came out of sleep and into wakefulness with." In common with 'Compass', this was another Crosby song of hope, and a personal catechism detailing the way pain can be turned to therapeutic or cathartic advantage.

AFTER THE DOLPHIN

Despite the title this was nothing to do with dolphins at all. Instead of the anticipated ecological warning in the vein of 'Wind On The Water' or 'Barrel Of Pain', this was about the destruction of a London pub called the Dolphin, back in 1915. According to Nash's research, the Dolphin pub, situated in the East End, was the first civilian target by enemy aircraft during the First World War, resulting in the deaths of seven people. The frightening randomness of death by bombing inspired Nash to produce one of his best compositions. This was a cut above virtually all the other tracks on the album. The use of radio broadcasts for eerie dramatic effect was particularly impressive. As Nash concluded: "I think that the juxtaposition between thinking that God is on your side in providing you with this weapon and the mass destruction it creates is really interesting... I find it difficult to understand that."

STEPHEN STILLS

STILLS ALONE

ORIGINAL RELEASE DATE: AUGUST 1991

With no prospects of issuing a new solo album on a major label, Stills turned to the independent circuit for this release, manufactured and distributed by Florida's Vision Records. Essentially, this was Stephen Stills Unplugged, but without the power and excitement of old. At times his vocals sounded tired and strained and his playing fair rather than spectacular. Although it was a welcome experience to hear Stills playing acoustic, he was let down by much of the material and the apparently half-hearted approach to the project. It was clear that Stills regarded this as an interim release and it was difficult to avoid the impression that he was wary of including too many good original songs in case he might need them for a more important project. The originals on offer were reasonably good, but far from outstanding, and Stills was careful to dig into his archives for older songs from his glory days at the beginning of the Seventies. Overall, the album lacked the invention and sparkle that it might have achieved and the running time of 35 minutes was decidedly stingy in the CD age.

ISN'T IT SO

A promising start to a long-awaited album, with a decent melody and well-played acoustic guitar. Stills' ability to pen a good ballad was evident, but in strangely small doses.

EVERYBODY'S TALKIN'

Stills was a great admirer of Fred Neil, whose composition was made famous by Nilsson. Unfortunately, this track had already been recorded by Stills for his live album back in 1975. Although this version was adequate, with a tired vocal which arguably reflected the sentiments of the song, its justification as an album track was dubious.

JUST ISN'T LIKE YOU

Despite a momentary uplifting slide break in the middle of the song, this was below average fare from Stills, with a noticeably weak melody.

IN MY LIFE

Lennon/McCartney's classic made famous on *Rubber Soul* had previously been covered with some success by Stills' former paramour Judy Collins. Stills' version sounded weary but likeable, although it would later be covered more successfully by CS&N.

THE BALLAD OF HOLLIS BROWN

Stills enjoyed playing the bluesman on Dylan's ballad of the downtrodden, which had appeared on his third album, *The Times They Are A-Changin'*. Stills' version is faithful, but wearisome.

SINGIN' CALL

This rough acoustic version of a song already familiar from *Stephen Stills 2* was another questionable choice, although it fitted in with the general bleak mood of the album.

THE RIGHT CALL

Another understated production, this time in the form of a country ballad. Not a great song by Stills' standards, but at least welcome amid the cover material on the album.

BLIND FIDDLER MEDLEY

An intriguing blues, in which Stills combined the traditional 'Blind Fiddler' with two of his familiar classics 'Do For The Others' and 'Know You Got To Run' (from *Stephen Stills* and *Stephen Stills 2* , respectively).

AMAZONIA

Probably the most uplifting track on the album, this ecological reflection on the state of the Amazon rain forests enabled Stills to show off his Latin American musical roots. His acoustic playing was also impressive.

TREETOP FLYER

This tale of a Vietnam veteran flyer turned smuggler was another old Stills composition that he had never got round to including on an album. Its appearance was welcome, though some saw it as further evidence of a lack of new songs.

THOUSAND ROADS

David Crosby

DAVID CROSBY

THOUSAND ROADS

ORIGINAL RELEASE DATE: APRIL 1993

Crosby's songwriting output was always slight in comparison to the other members of CSN&Y and it was partly for this reason that he elected to record an album of covers. Strangely, he also decided not to play any instruments on the album. "Bonnie Raitt was my inspiration for that," he noted. "I saw her making records where she only wrote one or two tunes, yet the whole record felt like Bonnie. 'Hey,' I told myself, 'the girl knows something, there's something to be learned here'." While the prospect of Crosby reinventing himself as an interpretative singer was an interesting conceit, the results were less than riveting. Fans missed his songwriting and distinctive guitar playing, while the deliberately contemporary production made some of the songs sound sterile and unconvincing. If the album had broken through commercially, then Crosby would have been in a strong position to relaunch his solo career, but its failure led him back into the shadows, with CS&N as his most likely vehicle for new product.

HERO

Co-written by Phil Collins, who also produced the track and played keyboards and drums, this was the first song recorded for the album. Crosby had previously guested on Collins' 'Another Day In Paradise' and 'That's Just The Way It Is' and their collaboration developed via the transatlantic fax, with Phil acting as a sounding board and editor in helping Crosby complete the music and lyrics. "Eventually he sends me this demo that was amazing," Crosby enthused. "You could have put that out. It would have been a hit... He came here when I was in a wheelchair and stuff and went out of his way to be a friend to me and come and visit and cheer me up. He was very generous; he produced it, he sang it, he was even in the video. He did everything he could to make it a success. I'm extremely grateful to him because I don't know anything about making singles." Although the vocal pairing was a decidedly uneasy mix, this was the closest Crosby was likely to reach in securing a radio hit.

TOO YOUNG TO DIE

Produced by Don Was, this was written by Jimmy Webb, who also guested on piano. What seemed a nostalgic car song of average quality, clearly struck a greater chord with Crosby. "I asked Jimmy for a song and he sent me that tape and I thought he must have sent me the wrong tape," he marvelled. "I thought, 'Nobody would give away this song. No one would let you have a chance at a song like this. It's just not in the cards...' J.D. Souther, Don Henley and I sang back-up vocals on his version of it and he came and played piano on my version of it."

OLD SOLDIER

Crosby first met Marc Cohn at the Grammy Awards ceremony when the latter won Best

New Artiste. "I had just listened to his record," Crosby explains, "and I thought he was a stunner. I think Marc's one of the first real singer-songwriters to come along in a long time". Cohn duly agreed to produce the song and play piano, with Graham Nash adding harmonies. The result was one of the better songs on the album.

THROUGH YOUR HANDS

Producer Don Was suggested Crosby should cover this John Hiatt song. Although the track was quite good, there was a distinct AOR feel with a tendency towards slickness at the expense of emotion.

YVETTE IN ENGLISH

The most important track on the album, this was a long-awaited collaboration between Crosby and his favourite songwriter, Joni Mitchell. Dean Parks co-produced the track, as well as playing guitar and flute. The song began as an incomplete lyric that Crosby wrote in a rent-a-car whilst driving from Tokyo to Narita Airport. Later, when he contacted Joni Mitchell about the possibility of contributing a song to this album, she responded, "Let's write one together." Crosby sheepishly presented the words and melody he had composed in his car and Mitchell responded enthusiastically. She provided the title 'Yvette In English' and added her unique observational touches to the lyric, adding depth to the composition and enhancing the mood. As Crosby recalled for *Song Talk*'s Paul Zollo: "She called me back and read me off her first rewrite of them on to my answering machine, which I should have saved because I was blown out of the water... Then she rewrote them more. She's a great craftsman as well as a great artist. She came back with it and I was just full of excitement. It was so good I couldn't believe it. She had melody and changes. And I changed the melody some when I recorded it, and the changes a little bit. It was just a very happy circumstance. And this is the best part: she liked it well enough that she recorded it too."

THOUSAND ROADS

Crosby wrote this in spontaneous fashion, then presented it to producer Glyn Johns who recruited Andy Fairweather Low to add some bluesy guitar. It's an odd and less than successful fusion of often incompatible talents.

COLUMBUS

This Noel Brazil composition had an obvious affinity with Crosby's songs of the sea like 'It Happens Each Day' and 'The Lee Shore'. "The nautical images and the way that they were overlaid as metaphors for things in life just thrilled me," Crosby concluded.

HELPLESS HEART

Producer Don Was was again in charge for this Paul Brady song, which was quite impressive despite a slightly schmaltzy string arrangement. "Phil Collins turned me on to 'Helpless Heart'," Crosby revealed. "He played it for me and said, 'If I was doing a record, I'd cut this'. I fell completely in love with it."

COVERAGE

Crosby's sole production on the album was this slightly neurotic song about radio and media fixation. The effects on Crosby's voice attract attention, as does the quirky lyric and amusing stabs at modernity.

NATALIE

Stephen Bishop's diary of a love affair won and lost provided a suitably plaintive conclusion to Crosby's covers album. "I went to Stephen Bishop looking for songs because I've always liked his chord changes and melodic feel," Crosby noted. "I know 'Natalie' is a tear-jerker, but it was too close to home for me not to record it. It works on any love-lost level, but if you listen to it carefully you'll realize that the girl in the song OD'd. I've lost a lot of people that way and it rang bells pretty strongly."

CROSBY, STILLS & NASH

AFTER THE STORM

ORIGINAL RELEASE DATE: AUGUST 1994

With Glyn Johns employed as producer, CS&N decided to concentrate on their strengths as songwriters, musicians and vocalists, without the uneasy attempts at modernity which blighted much of *Live It Up*. What emerged was nothing less than their first truly unified album since *CSN* 17 years before. On the trio's previous two albums, either Crosby or Stills had arrived late in the proceedings and a duet album had been artificially transformed into a three-way effort. This time, they were unified from the outset and the song allocation was the fairest on offer to date. David Crosby was involved in four of the 12 songs as a composer – the first time he had ever approached equality in the songwriting stakes. Nash remained his old buoyant self and, most remarkably, Stills emerged from what seemed a creative fog to offer some strong material with a noticeably improved singing voice. Although not every track was a stunner, the album underlined that when CS&N were all functioning properly and in harmony, they were still capable of producing work of power and considerable promise.

ONLY WAITING FOR YOU

A strong, upbeat opening from Stills, with some humorous lines, including the revelation that his younger self was "a basket case". After the synth rock experimentation of *Live It Up*, it was a relief to hear those familiar CS&N harmonies in isolation and more gratifying still to witness Stills' return as a confident vocalist and formidable acoustic player.

FIND A DREAM

In a new show of solidarity, Stills and Nash alternate lead vocals on this track, which also features James "Hutch" Hutchinson on chunky bass guitar, and Graham on harmonica and piano. Composed entirely by Nash, the song reflects obliquely on life, time and people in separate stanzas.

CAMERA

This rare songwriting collaboration between Crosby and Stills was their first attempt to write together exclusively since the glory days of 'Wooden Ships'. Crosby echoed Christopher Isherwood's "I Am A Camera" with the happy illusion of freezing time. There was also a passing reference to David's father, cinematographer Floyd Crosby and his work in South America. The intelligent lyrics were complemented by a surprise musical backing, featuring Alexis Sklarevski (bass), Tristan Imboden (drums) and Rafael Padilla (percussion).

UNEQUAL LOVE

This strictly no-frills Nash song, featured the composer on acoustic guitar and harmonica, with Benmont Tench on Hammond B-3 and Stills providing some carefully played lead guitar. Nash's lyrics on the sadness of unequal love recalled the thematic concerns of parts of

his first album, although the words were less self-conscious.

TILL IT SHINES ON YOU

With Stills on electric lead and some funky bass from James "Hutch" Hutchinson, a bluesy-voiced Crosby offers some passing observations on misinformation and self-awareness. The lyrics were elliptical but, like several of Crosby's recent blues-based outings, the song was not one of his best.

IT WON'T GO AWAY

Stills' legendary reputation as Captain Manyhands was reinforced by this upbeat number on which he played bass guitar, electric lead, and sang. Lyrically, the concerns were racial prejudice and media hypocrisy, themes familiar to the man who once wrote 'Word Game'.

THESE EMPTY DAYS

Stills and Ethan Johns traded chords on acoustic guitar while Stephen's son Christopher appeared on piano. Nash provided the mournful lyrics, with Stills prominent in the counter harmonies.

IN MY LIFE

Alas, this was already familiar having appeared on Stephen's downmarket solo album, *Stills Alone*. Fortunately, this was a much better version, made more powerful by the CS&N harmonies, which recalled their previous grand work when covering The Beatles' 'Blackbird'. Stills' voice had improved noticeably since *Stills Alone*, and his acoustic playing was as strong as ever, with his son Christopher adding some high string acoustic guitar and Ethan Jones on mandocello.

STREET TO LEAN ON

Crosby turned social commentator here, reflecting on urban life, street gangs and the state of the homeless. He even introduced non-American listeners to a new word, "galleria". The familiar crew of James "Hutch" Hutchinson (bass), Michael Hedges (acoustic guitar) and Michael Finnigan (keyboards), provided a sprightly backing.

BAD BOYZ

Like Crosby, Stills also turned to social commentary with this aggressive musical take on street gangs and the current fad for carrying guns. It was intriguing to witness CS&N suddenly moving away from the old themes of personal relationships, ecology and radical politics towards vibrant songs on everyday social problems.

AFTER THE STORM

Nash's love of meteorological imagery as a symbol of unrest was last heard on 'Grave Concern' on his second album. Here, the musical execution was not dissimilar, but this time the theme was personal rather than political. Nash plays harmonica, while Jennifer Stills appears as an additional vocalist.

PANAMA

With son Christopher Stills on Spanish guitar, Stephen recounts his social and sexual awakening as a 15-year-old in Panama. His personal voyage of discovery emerges as the highlight of the album. Easily the best

Latin-influenced song he had composed since 'Pensamiento' during the Manassas days, this irresistible musical excursion benefited from the contributions of Alexis Sklarevski (bass), Tristan Imboden (drums), Rafael Padilla (percussion) and Joe Rotondi (keyboards). A great conclusion to the album and a welcome return for Stills at his musical and lyrical best.

DAVID CROSBY

It's all coming back to me now...

DAVID CROSBY

IT'S ALL COMING BACK TO ME NOW...

ORIGINAL RELEASE DATE: JANUARY 1995

There was a time in the mid-Eighties when the prospect of a David Crosby live recording seemed more likely to be a posthumous release rather than a new album. A decade on from his drug rehabilitation, this was a welcome and unexpected opportunity to enjoy a solo concert, recorded at Hollywood's Whisky A Go Go on 7 December 1993. Backed by guitarist Jeff Pevar, bassist James "Hutch" Hutchinson, keyboardist Michael Finnigan and drummer Jody Cortez, Crosby presented a set of familiar classics and some recent recordings. The acoustic section began with a beautifully sung version of 'In My Dreams', which demonstrated how well Crosby's voice had survived years of freebasing abuse. An excellent 'Hero', included Kipp Lennon from the vocal group Venice on harmony and compared favourably with the slicker version on 1993's *Thousand Roads*. There was also a preview of 'Till It Shines On You', a year before its inclusion on *After The Storm*. The one song unique to this collection was 'Rusty And Blue', a six-minute meditation, featuring some striking acoustic guitar.

The second half of the album was an electric set, dominated by 25-year-old songs. After a lengthy, blues-based version of 'Cowboy Movie', Crosby invited special guest Chris Robinson from The Black Crowes to sing alternate lead on a spiky version of 'Almost Cut My Hair'. Finally, old friend Graham Nash took the stage for a spooky reading of 'Déjà Vu', which included bass, harmonica and guitar solos, before the familiar finale 'Wooden Ships' ended the evening.

Although only a minor release, predominantly aimed at dedicated fans, this was a pleasing memento at a time when solo releases from Crosby, Stills or Nash were seemingly no longer deemed commercially viable.

Full track listing: In My Dreams; Rusty And Blue; Hero; Till It Shines On You; Thousand Roads; Cowboy Movie; Almost Cut My Hair; Déjà Vu; Long Time Gone; Wooden Ships.

DAVID CROSBY

KING BISCUIT
FLOWER HOUR

RECORDS

DAVID CROSBY

DAVID CROSBY

ORIGINAL RELEASE DATE: AUGUST 1996

Released officially by King Biscuit Flower Hour Records, this was recorded at the Tower Theater, Philadelphia on 8 April 1989 and featured Crosby playing acoustic guitar, plus a band comprising Michael Finnigan (keyboards, vocals), Dan Dugmore (guitar), Davey Farragher (bass, vocals) and Jody Cortez (drums). "I remember that it was a very good show," Crosby recalled. "That was a really good band. The way I remember it, we were good almost all the time on that tour. I am being very unhumble here, but it really was a great band and that show, in particular, was very strong. We came away from it thinking, 'we really lucked out'. We were doing this for millions of listeners on the King Biscuit Flower Hour, and nobody screwed up and we really played great." Crosby's testimonial is not borne out by a close listening to the CD. At the time, he was promoting *Oh Yes I Can* which, not unexpectedly, dominates the track listing. Not long out of jail, Crosby was still having trouble finding the smooth texture once associated with his voice. Some of the acoustic songs here make for painful listening, with 'In My Dreams' sounding particularly coarse, hoarse and off-key. Towards the end of the electric set, this roughness works to his advantage on 'Nighttime For The Generals' and 'Almost Cut My Hair'. Although not the ideal live recording to release in 1996, especially immediately following *It's All Coming Back To Me Now...*, this package at least offered value for money with a full concert, 74 minutes in length.

Full track listing: Tracks In The Dust; Guinnevere; Compass; In My Dreams; Drive My Car; Lady Of The Harbor; Oh Yes I Can; Monkey And The Underdog; Delta; Déjà Vu; Nighttime For The Generals; Wooden Ships; Almost Cut My Hair; Long Time Gone.

Crosby - Nash

Another Stoney Evening

CROSBY – NASH

ANOTHER STONEY EVENING

ORIGINAL RELEASE DATE: JANUARY 1998

The recent upsurge in archive related Crosby material culminated in this special offering. Originally recorded at LA's Dorothy Chandler Pavilion on 10 October 1971, this release was inspired by the famous *A Very Stony Evening*, a bootleg double album taken from another show at the same venue. Hearing Crosby & Nash at the time of their greatest glory is a welcome experience. Part of the charm of this work lay in the stoned humour with which the duo conducted their concerts. Crosby joked that they were the loosest musicians in the world, but their performance gives the lie to that viewpoint. Beneath the easy-going comedy, the music was deadly serious. The acoustic playing, brilliantly captured here in an enchanting production, showed the duo at an all-time peak. Many of the songs featured were still unissued at the time, which made the selection sound even more impressive. Singling out individual tracks would prove a disservice to a record whose true power lies in its overall mood. For completists all that was missing were those sterling encore songs: 'Ohio', 'Military Madness' and 'Chicago'. For those of us who prized and over-played our bootleg versions of *A Very Stony Evening*, this was the ultimate surprise present, lovingly compiled, and superbly produced by Stephen Barncard. Those fortunate enough to have attended these concerts witnessed a crucially important chapter in the history of the group. Although there were many bigger concerts featuring the full CSN&Y line-up, this was as close as you could get to the true spirit of their work. The acoustic set highlights songs that are stripped to the core, leaving a lasting impression of exquisite harmonies and exemplary playing. This unexpected and most gratifying release is a testament to some unforgettable work, the like of which we are never likely to hear again.

Full track listing: Déjà Vu; Wooden Ships; Man In The Mirror; Orleans; Used To Be A King; Traction In The Rain; Lee Shore; Southbound Train; Laughing; Triad; Where Will I Be; Strangers Room; Immigration Man; Guinnevere; Teach Your Children.

COMPILATIONS

Below is a brief chronological survey of the compilations issued by the CSN&Y family, excluding Neil Young's *Decade*, full details of which were included in the Neil Young volume in this series.

CROSBY, STILLS, NASH & YOUNG

SO FAR

ORIGINAL RELEASE DATE: JULY 1974.

When CSN&Y reconvened in 1974 for their celebrated stadium tour, their record company and fans were crying out for new product. The foursome declined the opportunity to record a new album, much to everyone's frustration, and so this compilation was hastily issued. It warrants a mention here for two reasons: first, it was a number 1 album and is still available on CD; second, it featured the single version of 'Ohio'/'Find The Cost Of Freedom', compositions that are crucially important in any discussion of CSN&Y.

Those two features notwithstanding, there is little else to recommend the collection. The idea of releasing a compilation album from an act that had only recorded a single studio album as a foursome and another as a trio (minus Young) was stretching the meaning of the album title to absurd lengths. None of the four took the project seriously and were clearly embarrassed by its existence, although its chart performance must have been gratifying for all. At least Joni Mitchell provided some originality by providing the artwork.

OHIO

CSN&Y'S greatest moment on record was this moving anthem dedicated to the four students killed by the National Guard at Kent State University on 4 May 1970. At the time

Young seemed an apolitical creature but it was difficult to sit on the fence amid the ever present liberal radicalism of CS&N. Crosby, one of the great proselytizers in rock, was the catalyst in encouraging Young to react to the Kent State killings. He even gave him the press report of the event and watched solicitously as Young rapidly wrote the composition. "It was done in one day," Crosby told me. "Neil and I were sitting in Butano Canyon up north. I handed him *Life* magazine with a report of the Kent State killings. He read the article, picked up the guitar and started writing the song. I watched him write it. He and I then got on the plane, went to Los Angeles, went into the studio with Stills & Nash and made the record." The song's sentiments were uncompromising and finger-pointing ("Tin soldiers and Nixon's coming/We're finally on our own/This summer I hear the drumming/Four dead in Ohio"). CSN&Y, then scattered, immediately reconvened in LA and recorded the song, which was backed by Stills' 'Find The Cost Of Freedom'. Using their power and influence at Atlantic, CSN&Y ensured that the record was in the shops by the following week. The single still sounds staggering with Young's searing guitar

work illuminating a brilliant live performance which concludes with Crosby screaming "How many more? Why?" with such passion that he can barely hold back the tears. This unforgettable moment underlined everything that CSN&Y meant at their peak.

FIND THE COST OF FREEDOM

This served as the anthemic finale for CSN&Y's concert performances. The single version, included here, was a short but startling composition, which Stills had originally written for inclusion in the movie *Easy Rider* at the request of Dennis Hopper. Regrettably, Hopper passed on the song, much to Stills' mortification. The song remains one of the most moving and powerful statements of its time and a fitting requiem for all that CSN&Y represented.

Full track listing: Déjà Vu; Helplessly Hoping; Wooden Ships; Teach Your Children; Ohio; Find The Cost Of Freedom; Woodstock; Our House; Helpless; Guinnevere; Suite: Judy Blue Eyes.

STEPHEN STILLS

STILL STILLS: THE BEST OF STEPHEN STILLS

ORIGINAL RELEASE DATE: DECEMBER 1976

This half-hearted release was designed to cash in on the Christmas market and was largely unheralded as a result. Chaotically ordered, it included snapshots from Stills' two solo albums and the first Manassas release.

Full track listing: Love The One You're With; It Doesn't Matter; We Are Not Helpless; Marianne; Bound To Fall; Isn't About Time; Change Partners; Go Back Home; Johnny's Garden; Song Of Love; Sit Yourself Down.

Love Work Out · The Wall Song · Wild Tales · Carry Me · Out Of The Darkness

The best of David Crosby and Graham Nash

Southbound Train · Laughing · Chicago · Bittersweet · To The Last Whale

CROSBY NASH

CROSBY & NASH

THE BEST OF DAVID CROSBY & GRAHAM NASH

ORIGINAL RELEASE DATE: OCTOBER 1978

This seemed little more than a tired and cynical exercise in recycling from a disgruntled record company featuring indiscriminate selections from Crosby & Nash's albums, Nash's two albums and Crosby's solo work. Even the selection looked a mess.

Full track listing: Love Work Out; The Wall Song; Wild Tales; Carry Me; Out Of The Darkness; Southbound Train; Laughing; Chicago: Bittersweet; To The Last Whale... A. Critical Mass, B. Wind On The Water.

David *Stephen* *Graham*
CROSBY & STILLS AND NASH

PLAYREPLAYREPLAYREPLAYREPLAYRE

CROSBY, STILLS & NASH

REPLAY

ORIGINAL RELEASE DATE: DECEMBER 1980

Compiled under protest from Stills and Nash when Atlantic demanded a compilation for the Christmas market, this was an unnecessary and unimpressive release. Stills attempted some surgery on the record, removing the strings from 'I Give You Give Blind' and recutting 'Carry On' with Billy Meeker on drums. The 'Questions' segment was removed from 'Carry On', and Neil Young's guitar work was deleted.

Full track listing: Carry On; Marrakesh Express; Just A Song Before I Go; First Things First; Shadow Captain; To The Last Whale... A. Critical Mass, B. Wind On The Water; Love The One You're With; Pre-Road Downs; Change Partners; I Give You Give Blind; Cathedral.

· CROSBY, STILLS & NASH · CROSBY, STILLS, NASH & YOUNG ·
CROSBY & NASH · DAVID CROSBY · GRAHAM NASH · STEPHEN STILLS
· MANASSAS · CROSBY STILLS & NASH · STEPHEN STILLS ·
MANASSAS · CROSBY & NASH · DAVID CROSBY · GRAHAM NASH
CSN

CROSBY, STILLS & NASH
CSN Box Set
ORIGINAL RELEASE DATE: DECEMBER 1991

Undoubtedly one of the best box sets ever released, this sumptuous package boasted 77 tracks, including five previously unissued titles and a wealth of alternate takes, demos and different mixes. Graham Nash was the major player in the project and ensured that the selection was democratic and well-chosen. There are countless examples of immense care being taken to ensure that unedited takes and rarities are included, while the packaging and booklet are excellent. The following is a breakdown of the 25 recordings exclusive to the box set.

SUITE: JUDY BLUE EYES

This alternate mix was most notable for the inclusion of Dallas Taylor on drums. It was a far-sighted decision from CS&N to reject this in favour of the superior, pure acoustic version. Although the box set notes refer to this merely as a different mix, the vocal is also different in places, most notably the "tearing yourself away from me now" verse. After singing the high part ending with "thrill me to the marrow", Nash is so enchanted by the power of the performance that he exclaims, "beautiful".

HELPLESSLY HOPING

An unreleased live studio version from CSN&Y, this was recorded on 15 June 1969 around the time of the release of the first CS&N album. At one point, they intended to feature a steel guitar on the track, but Stills effectively duplicated the sound. This version was also notable for the inclusion of three ex-members of Buffalo Springfield: Stills, Young and bassist Bruce Palmer.

YOU DON'T HAVE TO CRY

Recorded at the Record Plant, New York, in December 1968, this early take was a lot more country-influenced than the released version, with Stills playing a Chet Atkins' Country Gentleman guitar.

GUINNEVERE

This was recorded before the formation of CS&N at United Studio B, Hollywood on 26 June 1968, with Jack Casady on bass and Cyrus Faryar on bouzouki. Intriguing as the origins of a new sound that would soon change popular music, this early version revealed Crosby's folk roots, with a feel that brought out the mystery of the song even more prominently than the released version.

BLACKBIRD

Beginning with Stills' schoolmasterly instructions, this was a great version of The Beatles' minor classic and a perfect song for three-part harmonies. A live favourite from their early concerts, it was revived at various points along the way.

SONG WITH NO WORDS (TREE WITH NO LEAVES)

Recorded by Crosby & Nash on 22 February 1971, this lacked the power of the brilliant version on *If I Could Only Remember My Name*. Nevertheless, it was a more than welcome addition to the box set, with Crosby's 12-string acoustic guitar prominent.

ALMOST CUT MY HAIR

Crosby's admonitions lead in one of the most intense songs on the box set. This was the full, unedited version, heard for the first time on record. Crosby, Stills and Young contribute the jagged guitar work – a highlight of this track.

HORSES THROUGH A RAINSTORM

Recorded on 28 December 1969, this Nash/Terry Reid collaboration featured the full CSN&Y line-up. The sound is very reminiscent of The Hollies. As Nash concluded: "In the end it smacked a little too much of the pop prisons from which we had all just escaped."

4+20

This was an alternate mix, although the differences sound minimal.

WOODSTOCK

A clearer alternate mix of the *Déjà Vu* track.

THE LEE SHORE

Another CSN&Y track, recorded on 28 December 1969. This was an outside contender for *Déjà Vu* that later appeared in more subdued acoustic form on the live album, *4 Way Street*. It's strange to hear such a delicate ballad given the full CSN&Y electric treatment. Nash's organ work is a little overbearing, while Stills' electric solo adds a different ambience to the track.

MAN IN THE MIRROR

Recorded live at the Fillmore East on 7 June 1970, this featured Crosby, Nash and Young on a pleasing version of the song later included on *Songs For Beginners*.

BLACK QUEEN

Another Fillmore live cut, described by Stills as "a country blues... a little music from back home". At one point, he even reprimands the audience for their levity before launching into a strong and less frantic reading of the released studio version.

URGE FOR GOING

This 1966 Joni Mitchell composition was attempted by Crosby & Nash on 22 June 1971, with each singer taking a verse. The sound was very much like a late Sixties' recording and an interesting counterpoint to their familiar singer-songwriter material.

SIMPLE MAN

This alternate mix generally displayed greater clarity, bringing out the cello backing of Dorian Rudnytsky and vibes accompaniment of Rita Coolidge.

MY LOVE IS A GENTLE THING

This previously unreleased Stills song was written in Hawaii. "I was thinking of the tropics as a woman," he observed. A slight ballad, barely over a minute long, it was a pleasing fragment to hear after all these years.

SEE THE CHANGES

This was the unreleased CSN&Y version, recorded at Young's Broken Arrow ranch on 28 June 1973, with Tim Drummond (bass), Joe Lala (congas) and Russ Kunkel (drums). Still in the rough stages, it inevitably lacked the power of the polished version later recorded by CS&N for their 1977 album.

HOMEWARD THROUGH THE HAZE

Re-recorded by Crosby & Nash, this is the original CSN&Y version cut at the Record Plant, Sausalito, on 16 December 1974. An exceptionally strong recording, this was the start of what should have been a great CSN&Y record that was ludicrously abandoned. The excellent guitar work of Stills and Young here is just one reminder of all that had been lost.

TAKEN AT ALL

Another doomed CSN&Y get-together, this time at Criteria Studios, Miami, on 1 April 1976. Nash later claimed that this was his all-time favourite CSN&Y track. Its power lies in the simple intensity of four acoustic guitars and four vocals working in unison. This song of lost opportunities was most appropriate given the sabotaging of the project after its recording.

WILD TALES

This live version, recorded at the Universal Amphitheatre on 3 August 1979, was a reminder of the period when Nash performed as a soloist.

DEAR MR FANTASY

Originally recorded by CS&N in 1970, this was a version cut 10 years later by Stills & Nash. The idea of CS&N covering a Traffic song was not so strange as Stills had once invited Stevie Winwood to join the unit as keyboardist. Despite Stills' obvious enthusiasm, this track would probably not have fitted well into the CSN&Y canon, although it remains an interesting cover.

GOT IT MADE

Recorded at the United Nations Assembly Hall, New York, in 1989, this was a stripped-down version of the Stills' song included on *American Dream*. Nash strikes some drum sticks together to add a minimalist, and slightly irritating rhythm.

AS I COME OF AGE

Dating from 1981, this was CS&N bravely tackling one of the finest songs on the excellent *Stills*. Slightly slower than the original, it was nonetheless a very strong version with a fine guitar solo from Stills and a sense of real maturity in the lyrical execution.

DRIVE MY CAR

Recorded at the Sound Labs, LA, in 1978, this was a tentative early version of a song intended for Crosby's doomed solo album in 1981 and later re-recorded for *Oh Yes I Can*. Given their involvement here, it begs the question of why they refused to allow the song to be featured on *Daylight Again*, where Crosby's presence was kept to a songwriting minimum.

SOLDIERS OF PEACE

An alternate CSN&Y take of a song destined for *American Dream*. Although less intense than the released version, this was still a powerful rendition and a worthy addition to the box.

Full track listing: Suite: Judy Blue Eyes; Helplessly Hoping; You Don't Have To Cry; Wooden Ships; Guinnevere; Marrakesh Express; Long Time Gone; Blackbird; Lady Of The Island; Song With No Words (Tree With No Leaves); Almost Cut My Hair; Teach Your Children; Horses Through A Rainstorm; Déjà Vu; Helpless; 4+20; Laughing; Carry On/Questions; Woodstock; Ohio; Love The One You're With; Our House; Old Times Good Times; The Lee Shore; Music Is Love; I'd Swear There Was Somebody Here; Man In The Mirror; Black Queen; Military Madness; Urge For Going; I Used To Be A King; Simple Man; Southbound Train; Change Partners; My Love Is A Gentle Thing; Word Game; Johnny's Garden; So Begins The Task; Turn Back The Pages; See The Changes; It

Doesn't Matter; Immigration Man; Chicago/We Can Change The World; Homeward Through The Haze; Where Will I Be?; Page 43; Carry Me; Cowboy Of Dreams; Bittersweet; To The Last Whale: A. Critical Mass B. Wind On The Water; Prison Song; Another Sleep Song; Taken At All; In My Dreams; Just A Song Before I Go; Shadow Captain; Dark Star; Cathedral; Wasted On The Way; Barrel Of Pain (Half-Life); Southern Cross; Daylight Again; Thoroughfare Gap; Wild Tales; Dear Mr Fantasy; Cold Rain; Got It Made; Tracks In The Dust; As I Come Of Age; 50/50; Drive My Car; Delta; Soldiers Of Peace; Yours And Mine; Haven't We Lost Enough?; After The Dolphin; Find The Cost Of Freedom.

RELATED RELEASES ROUND-UP

In addition to the above, otherwise unreleased CS&N/CSN&Y-related recordings have featured on a number of releases. The most famous of these is the triple album *Woodstock*, which included 'Suite: Judy Blue Eyes', 'Wooden Ships' and 'Sea Of Madness' (although it later emerged that the last track was not actually recorded at Woodstock, but taken from another date on the tour). CS&N also appeared on *Woodstock II*, which included '4+20', 'Marrakesh Express' and 'Guinnevere'. Neil Young and Graham Nash performed together on the 1972 single 'War Song'. A live version of CSN&Y's 'Pushed It Over The End' was released in Italy in 1982 on a 12-inch single, accompanying a box set. The album *No Nukes* featured CS&N performing 'You Don't Have To Cry', 'Long Time Gone' and 'Teach Your Children', plus Nash performing 'Cathedral', Nash and Jackson Browne on 'Crow On The Cradle', and Nash with James Taylor & Carly Simon on 'The Times They Are A-Changin''. The Various Artists' recording *Nintendo: White Knuckle Scorin'* included CS&N performing John Sebastian's 'How Have You Been'; the Various Artists' *Red Hot & Country* boasted a live 'Teach Your Children'; *Woodstock Diary* featured a live 'Blackbird' and *Woodstock '94* (US edition only) included 'Déjà Vu'. 'Chuck's Lament (A Child's Dream)' was available solely as a B-side, as was the A-side 'Chippin' Away'. Stills' otherwise unreleased 'Cuba Al Fin' can be heard on the Various Artists' *Havana Jam*. Nash's otherwise unavailable 'Love For A Reason' was on the soundtrack album, *Fast Times At Ridgmont High*. CSN&Y also appeared on *Woodstock: 25th Anniversary Box Set* performing 'Suite: Judy Blue Eyes', 'Find The Cost Of Freedom', 'Guinnevere', 'Marrakesh Express', '4+20' and 'Sea Of Madness' and Crosby can be heard singing the otherwise unavailable 'Fare Thee Well' on the B-side of his single, 'Hero'.

INDEX